New York University Studies
in Near Eastern Civilization
Number 10

General Editor
Bayly Winder

ALSO IN THIS SERIES

Number I: F. E. Peters, Aristotle and the Arabs

Number II: Jacob M. Landau, Jews in Nineteenth-Century Egypt

Number III: Lois Anita Giffen, Theory of Profane Love Among the Arabs: The Development of the Genre

Number IV: Lewis V. Thomas, A Study of Naima Norman Itkowitz, editor

Number V: Carl Max Kortepeter, Ottoman Imperialism During the Reformation: Europe and The Caucasus

Number VI: Linda Fish Compton, Andalusian Lyrical Poetry and Old Spanish Love Songs: The Muwashshah and Its Kharja

Number VII: Peter J. Chelkowski, Ta'ziyeh: Ritual and Drama in Iran

Number VIII: Arthur N. Young, Saudi Arabia: The Making of a Financial Giant

Number IX: Donald Quataert, Social Disintegration and Popular Resistance in the Ottoman Empire, 1881–1908: Reactions to European Economic Penetration

New York University Studies in Near Eastern Civilization

The participation of the New York University Press in the University's commitment to Near Eastern Studies provides Americans and others with new opportunities for understanding the Near East. Concerned with those various peoples of the Near East who, throughout the centuries, have dramatically shaped many of mankind's most fundamental concepts and who have always had high importance in practical affairs, this series, New York University Studies in Near Eastern Civilization, seeks to publish important works in this vital area. The purview will be broad, open to varied approaches and historical periods, including the range of social scientific approaches. It will, however, be particularly receptive to work in two areas that reflect the University and that may have received insufficient attention elsewhere. These are literature and art. Furthermore, taking a stand that may be more utilitarian than that of some other publications, the series will welcome translations of important Near Eastern literature. In this way, an audience, unacquainted with the languages of the Near East, will be able to deepen its knowledge of the cultural achievements of Near Eastern peoples.

Bayly Winder
General Editor

The Return of Consciousness

by

TAWFIQ AL-HAKIM

Translated from the Arabic by
BAYLY WINDER
Director, Hagop Kevorkian Center for Near Eastern Studies
Professor of History and of Near Eastern Languages and Literatures
New York University

NEW YORK UNIVERSITY PRESS
New York and London
1985

First Arabic edition June 1974
Second Arabic edition December 1974
First English edition 1985

First published 1985 in the USA by
NEW YORK UNIVERSITY PRESS
Washington Square, New York, NY 10003

Printed in Hong Kong

Library of Congress Cataloging in Publication Data

al-Hakim, Tawfiq.
The return of consciousness.

(New York University studies in Near Eastern civilization; no. 10)
Translation of: ‘Awdat al-wa‘i.
Includes bibliographical references and index.
1. Egypt – Politics and government – 1952–
I. Winder, R. Bayly (Richard Bayly), 1920–
II. Title. III. Series.
DT107.83.H334413 1984 962′.05 84-16670
ISBN 0–8147–9202–2

Contents

Translator's Introduction

President Jamal 'Abd al-Nasir, the leader of the Egyptian revolution of 1952 and the charismatic champion of militant Arab nationalism, died suddenly on 28 September 1970. Idolized, hated and feared in Egypt and throughout the Arab world, his legacy of hothouse nationalism and dictatorial brinkmanship seemed destined to dominate the Arab east for long years after his death. His regime had indubitably enabled Egyptians to hold their heads up after centuries of foreign domination, and constructive projects such as land reform and the building of the High Dam received much acclaim. On the other hand, the police-state methods, the disastrous wars with Israel and in Yemen, and the desperate domestic economy all combined to create a stifling atmosphere in which the upper classes were alienated and the urban masses, not to speak of the fellaheen, became increasingly torporous. Nevertheless, few imagined even as late as 1976 that the atmosphere would change so quickly that by 1977 President Anwar al-Sadat would deliver a speech to the Knesset in Jerusalem.

'Awdat al-Wa'i, *The Return of Consciousness*, the work here translated, is the intellectual forerunner of "Sadatism". It marks the first public, published repudiation of "Nasirism" to emerge from the upper-class, liberal, intelligentsian, Westernized sectors of Egyptian society.[1] As a published document it broke Egypt's group solidarity, and created a sensation. Its message is simple: We Egyptians were taken in by the promise of the revolution of 1952, and Jamal 'Abd al-Nasir, for all his personal charisma, imposed on us a police state which pursued failing policies in all directions. We, the intellectuals of Egypt, are to be rebuked for having accepted it all so passively at the time, but Egypt has now regained consciousness and can begin to move forward again.

Additional points are that for Tawfiq al-Hakim the revolution of 1919 against the British – the revolution of his generation – which ushered in democratic constitutional principles (no matter how poorly applied) and a decent concern for intellectual life, was the truly popular revolution. Finally, al-Hakim says that the secrets – the "file" as he calls it – of the 1952 revolution must be opened before a clear understanding of the achievements and, especially, the failures of the Nasirist regime can be objectively assessed.

'Awdat al-Wa'i was too hot to handle in Egypt when first published in June 1974 (the author dated the book on 23 July 1972) and hence appeared under a Beirut imprimatur. Even so, the reaction in Egypt, most vociferously from the left, was tremendous for a slender volume of some seventy-five pages. The second edition, translated here, contains some samples of this reaction, but they are mere samples.[2]

The explanation for the outcry is twofold. First, the cult of 'Abd al-Nasir was still much alive in the wake of his death, and al-Hakim, a well-established public figure in his own right, almost seemed guilty of treason in publicly condemning the practices and principles that had come close to constituting Egypt's inner identity from 1952 to 1970 and which as late as 1974, when the first edition appeared, were still part of the official iconography of the state.

There is a second reason for the high-pitched reaction. It is that many people felt that it ill became the author, who had willingly accepted position and rewards from the state during 'Abd al-Nasir's time and who indeed had publicly acclaimed President 'Abd al-Nasir, to wait until he was dead and then publicly attack him. The late Professor Muhammad al-Nuwayhi, of the American University in Cairo, in a private discussion of the matter quoted as applicable the following saying of the Prophet Muhammad: "He amongst you who sees an evil should change it with his hand; if he cannot, then with his tongue; and if he cannot, then with his heart. This last is the weakest kind of faith." That is to say, al-Hakim should have refrained from any relationship with the state during 'Abd al-Nasir's life or failing that have kept quiet after his death. Another thoughtful Egyptian observer made the following remark: "We agree with everything in *'Awdat al-Wa'i*, but it ill becomes Tawfiq to have written it when he received so much from the regime." The moral question posed is a serious one and not easy to brush away. Some of Tawfiq al-Hakim's own responses can be found at the back of the book.[3]

Tawfiq al-Hakim was born sometime around the turn of the century in Alexandria, the eldest son of a prosperous farmer/magistrate father and a mother of Turkish background who dominated the marriage. After studying in various schools, Tawfiq graduated in 1925 from the Cairo law school. But before that event two other forces had intruded heavily in his life. First, he had become totally wrapped up in every aspect of the nascent Egyptian theatre. He had written five plays by the time he received the law degree. Secondly, the revolution of 1919 against the British occupation had drawn in the young student and his uncles; Tawfiq was arrested for his part in it and imprisoned. This heady, youthful political participation made a deep and lasting impression as *'Awdat al-Wa'i*, and others of al-Hakim's works make very clear.

The next major phase of al-Hakim's life was his sojourn of some three years in Paris. On the advice of his father's friend, the well-known writer Lutfi al-Sayyid, Tawfiq was sent to study for a Ph.D. in law, "but in fact he was preparing himself for a career in theatre. He didn't go to any drama school, but he was studying independently, reading plays and about plays and seeing performances. . . . His intensive reading in Paris was not limited to drama."[4] In fact this voracious young man tasted, and not superficially, every aspect of Western culture from Beethoven to Edgar Allan Poe, and he fell in love with it. When his father finally forced him home, young Tawfiq suffered a very severe case of reverse culture shock. The pain was in the end sublimated in writing and by 1933 when *'Awdat al-Ruh*[5] and "Ahl al-Kahf"[6] had appeared he was an established figure in the modern Egyptian literary renaissance.

Al-Hakim's career started with a six-year period (1928–34) as a public prosecutor. For the next five years he served in the ministry of education and then, from 1939 to 1943, in the ministry of social affairs. He then left government service in order to devote himself to writing, but in 1951 he was made director of the national library, a post that he held until 1956 in which year he became a full-time member of the Higher Council of Arts, Literature and Social Science. During 1959–60 he was the Egyptian representative to UNESCO, returning later to his post at the Council of Arts. In recent years Tawfiq al-Hakim has been a writer on literature for *Al-Ahram*. In all, he has written some fifty plays and books.

It is perhaps of interest to set forth a few points that relate to Tawfiq al-Hakim's recognition by the state (in addition to employment) and his public pronouncements about 'Abd al-Nasir and his regime. He had already received official recognition before the revolution in that the title of "bey" had been conferred on him. Soon after the revolution he was elected to the national language academy, al-Majma' al-Lughawi, but a more signal honour came in 1958 when President 'Abd al-Nasir awarded Tawfiq the Qiladat al-Jumhuriyah (republican chain) – an honour previously reserved for eminent foreign leaders such as heads of state. In part the honour was recognition by President 'Abd al-Nasir of the impact that the novel *'Awdat al-Ruh* had had on him. The list goes on: in 1962 al-Hakim received the state prize for literature which carried an honorarium of £E2500. The citation credits al-Hakim with devotion to drama, with enkindling the spirit of national consciousness through his plays and fiction, and cites his concern for social progress and his criticism of corruption and injustice. A year later a state-owned theatre was named (most aptly) after al-Hakim. In 1964 he visited the High Dam and published a short play in *Al-Ahram*[7] praising the dam. He also effusively thanked the president for his patronage of the arts. On the eve of the 1967 war he wrote to encourage the fighting men and regretted that his age prevented him from joining them.[8] In a similar vein when war broke out he wrote an official-type patriotic poem in *Al-Ahram*.[9]

Given the number of official appointments that Tawfiq al-Hakim held and the official honours that he received, it is certainly in order to try to understand where he stood. Denys Johnson-Davies, a student of al-Hakim, has answered as follows:

> Tewfik Al Hakim has never been interested in political creeds and "isms". No Egyptian, however, particularly a writer can stand wholly aloof from politics. . . . Over the years [he] has shown great skill – not shared by many of his fellow authors – in keeping out of political trouble. The inevitable accusation of living in an ivory tower . . . has been levelled; while he has never entered any political arena, he has none the less throughout his career shown himself deeply concerned with such fundamental and potentially dangerous issues as justice and truth, good and evil and, above all, freedom.[10]

Other insightful critics of Tawfiq al-Hakim have interpreted this aspect of the writer less charitably; however, most of us do not decline honours from the president of our country, and most of us do not publish works of imaginative literature and expository writing that encourage foreign critics to write of our "preoccupation with freedom".[11]

Al-Hakim's merits as a writer hardly need to be addressed in a paragraph or two. Called in 1972 "probably the foremost imaginative writer of today's Arab world",[12] he along with Taha Husayn and others is one of something like a galaxy of Egyptian writers who shone in the inter-war period and beyond. He has been prolific as a dramatist (in drama al-Hakim stands alone), novelist, essayist, political thinker, satirist, critic and autobiographer. I shall content myself with some brief selective additions to the English-language bibliography on al-Hakim to supplement those titles given in the introduction to my translation of *'Usfur min al-Sharq*:[13]

Ali, Mohamed Hamed, "Philosophical Concepts in Five Plays by the Egyptian Dramatist Tawfik al-Hakim" (unpublished Ph.D. dissertation, University of Denver, 1968).

Barazanji, Ahmed Zeyad, "The Impact of European Drama on Two Arab Playwrights: Tawfiq al-Hakim and Kateb Yacine" (unpublished Ph.D. dissertation, City University of New York, 1979).

Bar-Nissim, Nahman, "Tawfiq Al-Hakim: The Dramatist" (unpublished Ph.D. dissertation, University of Pennsylvania, 1970).

Cooley, John K., "'We Must Do More': Tewfik al-Hakim: Egypt's Dean of Imagination, Author in Residence", *Christian Science Monitor*, 22 March 1972, p. 23.

Hakim, Tawfiq al-, "The Donkey Market", trans. by Denys Johnson-Davies, in D. Johnson-Davies, *Egyptian One-Act Plays* (London: Heinemann, 1981; Washington, D.C.: Three Continents Press, 1981).

——, *"Fate of a Cockroach" and Other Plays*, trans. by Denys Johnson-Davies (London: Heinemann, 1972).

——, *Plays, Prefaces, and Postscripts*, trans. by W. M. Hutchins (Washington, D.C.: Three Continents Press, 1981).

——, *"The Tree Climber": A Play*, trans. by Denys Johnson-Davies (London: Oxford University Press, 1966).

Khatib, Ibrahim Isma'il al-, "An Annotated Translation of the Play *Shahrazad* by Tawfiq al-Hakim" (unpublished Ph.D. dissertation, Southern Illinois University, 1969).

Long, Richard, *Tawfiq al-Hakim: Playwright of Egypt* (London: Ithaca Press, 1979).

Sakkūt, Ḥamdī, *The Egyptian Novel and its Main Trends from 1913 to 1951* (Cairo: The American University in Cairo Press, 1971) pp. 85–97.

Tutunji, Gilbert Victor, "Tawfiq al-Hakim and the West" (unpublished Ph.D. dissertation, Indiana University, 1966).

Wren, Christopher, "On Al Ahram's Sixth Floor", *New York Times Book Review*, 10 March 1980, pp. 3, 22–3.

Turning to the mechanics of the translation, I have followed the procedure of first putting down a literal version of the Arabic and then, with scant reference to the original, of attempting to put this first

English translation				Arabic text			
From		To		From		To	
page	line	page	line	page	line	page	line
8	13	8	25	21	– 5	22	5
17	1	17	10	34	7	34	14
20	16	20	18	38	– 3	38	– 1
21	– 8	21	– 7	40	– 9	40	– 8
21	– 5	22	1	40	– 6	40	– 1
23	19	23	26	43	3	43	9
24	– 1	25	1	45	5	43	5
27	25	27	33	49	6	49	12
27	– 3	27	– 1	49	– 7	49	– 6
28	1	28	2	49	– 5	49	– 4
29	15	29	24	51	– 3	52	5
29	– 9	30	2	52	–11	52	– 5
32	8	32	14	55	– 5	56	1
32	16	32	20	56	3	56	7
37	– 9	37	– 7	63	– 4	63	– 2
38	24	39	5	64	– 3	65	14
39	8	39	11	65	16	65	18
41	– 2	41	– 1	69	– 8	69	– 7
42	–12	45	3	70	– 7	73	– 4
45	13	45	15	74	6	74	7
45	–11	45	– 3	74	– 2	75	4
47	9	47	15	77	2	77	6
49	17	49	18	80	3	80	4
49	– 9	49	– 5	80	10	80	13
49	– 1	51	– 2	80	– 7	83	14
52	2	52	3	83	16	83	17
53	– 7	54	– 8	86	5	87	–6
55	11	55	21	88	7	88	14
56	1	56	–15	89	8	90	5
57	8	57	9	91	3	91	4

version into decent English. I have not pursued consistency in the rendering of a given word or phrase, but I have more or less controlled the renderings and have tried to vary them only with some cause. I have not hesitated (though I should perhaps have gone further) to suppress some of the "parallelisms" beloved of Arabic nor to add an odd English phrase if it seemed helpful. All the notes are mine; the general principle was to elucidate people, places, institutions, and events that might not be familiar to an ordinary literate reader of English. Many will be superfluous for specialists. Transliteration follows the Library of Congress system without diacritical marks. I have preferred to leave all Arabic titles in their original form, transliterated, rather than to invent translated titles, but each title is translated on its first occurrence in the relevant note. The index will allow the reader to recheck easily the meanings of titles.

There is one particular problem to note. It is the differences between the first and second editions of *'Awdat al-Wa'i*.[14] The first edition (Beirut: Dar al-Shuruq, June 1974) contains 76 pages; the second, just over 90. In other words, the second is some twenty per cent longer. The additions (there are no deletions) vary from small stylistic changes, to the addition of a sentence or a paragraph, to additions two or more pages long. In general, the additions seem to have constituted an attempt to justify further and elucidate al-Hakim's various contentions in the face of the blistering attacks made on the first edition. Obviously the sample of such attacks and al-Hakim's rebuttals both of which are appended to the second edition constitute a different kind of addition. So that the reader can judge the first type of addition, I chart the major ones opposite.

Several have helped me in this work whether as elucidators of difficult or unclear passages, typists, research assistants, proof-readers, or language improvers. These include: H. E. Ambassador Tahsin Bashir, Geraldine DiCicco, the late Professor Philip K. Hitti, Charles Issawi, Michel F. Le Gall, Sandra Levy, Ghassan Nakad and Mona Mikhail. I thank them all.

Most of all I want to express my appreciation to my wife, Viola, not only for helping in more or less all of the above categories, but also for helping in the really important ways.

New York University BAYLY WINDER

Preface to the Second Edition

After the appearance of the first edition of *'Awdat al-Wa'i* the Nasirists, both in Egypt and elsewhere, were angered and puffed and stormed as though Nasirism were a sacred religion which should not be touched or as though 'Abd al-Nasir were superhuman rather than a created being whose mistakes could be analysed. If the person of Jamal 'Abd al-Nasir were the point, then we would have the duty to be forbearing, and I would be the first to appeal for remembering him compassionately and for allowing him to rest in peace. I wish that this could be my position toward his person and his name, but 'Abd al-Nasir is not just a person and a name. In fact, he is a long period of rule which impressed on all of Egypt a definite stamp and which, since his departure, has continued to press on the body of Egypt as though it were a brand which had effaced all underlying characteristics. The days pass, and the generations rise, and one cannot tell what is under this stamp, or what existed before it, or what will come after it. Should Egypt, then, stop its political, intellectual and social development because it does not know or wish to discover the truth concerning this period of absolute personal rule? If we want Egypt to stand on its own two feet and walk by itself on the road to progress, there is no way to avoid opening up the whole file on the revolution of 1952 and examining the truth. It will not be necessary, after opening the file, to prosecute and punish. That is not a productive goal. The most important goal in what I call "opening up the file" is opening our eyes to the mistakes and disasters of the past so that we can avoid them and prevent anyone else from repeating them while we build Egypt anew. We must also open our ears to claimed attainments and accomplishments so that we can examine their true value and their actual results because in this period, which was full of lies, resonant but empty slogans were mixed in with policies which may have actually produced benefits.

But the Nasirists, that is those who for one reason or another climbed on the bandwagon of 'Abd al-Nasir, are frightened by the mere mention of the file not to speak of actually opening it. Why? I shall leave the answer to the intelligence of those who love truth, who want their country to be built on trust, and who have no special aim or weakness. But I shall not cease appealing for the files to be opened and for the truth to be uncovered no matter how angry some people might become.

I also thought that readers of this edition should look over a sample of the reactions (included at the end of the book) to this work, together with my rejoinders, in order to clarify the various positions and in the hope that each citizen will put the interest of his country above every other concern.

Foreword

I had no plan or intention to permit publication of these pages at the time I wrote them. What impelled me to write them at that time was the passage of twenty years since the revolution of 1952 plus my reflections on this period in the history of my country, especially since the atmosphere around me was then gloomy with painful events and since spirits were depressed by the nightmare of *the* defeat.

I began to retrace such pictures of the revolution and of my relationship to it as I still remembered, and while making an account of it, I also made an account of myself. I had informed no one of these pages. I preferred to insert them among my private papers and thus to preserve something which concerned me alone. I considered them memoirs which were not yet to be published but which delimited on paper my personal feelings about that considerable period of my life . . ., and that is what I did. I felt that, if possible, the positions of those whose opinions were to be published should be the positions which existed during and within the events – not after them. By way of contrast, had it only been a matter of recording memories, or reviewing yesterdays, and examining one's self, such writing would necessarily be possible only after the passage of the events in question. Thus these pages remained a secret manuscript until events willed on a certain occasion that I show them to an old friend in whom I had complete confidence. He asked permission to make a copy of my manuscript to keep for himself. He had one typed up, and, lo and behold, a number of copies showed up. Then they multiplied and spread secretly from hand to hand until the whole matter got out of my control. I did not pay much attention to what had happened or would happen because the original written in my hand was always in my possession, whereas neither my signature nor my name was on the copies which were circulating. However, the matter became serious when one day a respected French journal published an incomplete translation from one of those spreading *samizdat*. Then another European journal sought my permission to publish, but I refused, and it gave in to my will. Finally, I learned that a newspaper in Lebanon had translated the incomplete French version into an Arabic version which was far from the original both in style and in content. Subsequently, more than one publisher came to request publication of the complete original text, under my own name and in my own style, in one newspaper or another to be followed by its appearance in book form. At this point I decided to sue all those who had published these premature pages translated without my knowledge or permission and who had attributed them to me. However, after reflection and consultation with some well-informed and thoughtful friends, it became clear that bringing suit would end up as a disavowal of those pages in so far as they did express my opinion. In my friends' view such a denial was not in my nature; they had long known that I would never deny anything that I had written – or even something that I had not written but which had been attributed to me, in which I believed, and which I found to reflect my views. They agreed that I should admit authorship as long as the publication had in fact taken place. They thought that it was the people's right to read what I had written, whether secretly or openly, because the pen and thought were in their view the property of all the people and not the private, captive property of their creator. This view is sound, and it is also my belief. He who wields his pen and uses his brain is responsible for communicating to the people what he sees. This point is sound even though an author is not responsible for the soundness of his view, for he is clearly not guiltless in regard to faulty analysis, failure to see clearly, misunderstanding, soundness of judgement, or concealing the sources of knowledge. In addition, a writer is always responsible for the sincerity and truthfulness of his view as he sees it. Having recently given permission for the publication of these pages in full, I should like people to understand that they represent my views and my testimony to my conscience. I should not, however, want them to be taken as a political position or a final judgement. The reverse is the case. What I seek is objective research, careful investigation, and the uncovering of the truth – after opening the file of this period in its entirety.

The major task for the person who wields his pen and thinks is to expose the face of the truth.

TAWFIQ AL-HAKIM

‘Awdat al-Wa‘i
or
The Return of Consciousness

These lines are not history;
they are testimony and feelings
which I have brought forth from memory
and which are not based on any other source.

From Wednesday, 23 July 1952 to Sunday, 23 July 1972

The Return of Consciousness

I remember that it was Wednesday, for the following day, which was Thursday, was the day of my weekly trip to Alexandria. At that time I was the director of Dar al-Kutub.[1] My annual leave had not yet come, and my family had preceded me to our summer place so that I could spend the weekends with them. Thus I was alone at home and had no need for anyone to serve me, for I ate out and spent the evening with colleagues and friends who were writers and journalists. I didn't return to my apartment on Tuesday until the end of the evening and went straight to sleep. In those late July days Cairo was almost deserted. King Faruq had gone to Alexandria to his summer palace, al-Muntazah;[2] the government, along with its senior officials, had moved with him to its regular summer seat in Bulkeley.[3] Everything was proceeding its ordinary way. I returned home from my evening out and sought refuge in my bed.

THAT MORNING . . .

Early in the morning I got up and turned on the radio as I do every morning, but I heard something strange, the likes of which I had never heard before. It was a communiqué from the army announcing that it had staged an uprising in order to reform the corruption in the country. The communiqué further stated that the army would present demands to the royal palace in order to remove the king's corrupt entourage. Words in this sense I of course received with delight even if I did not read into them any more than they would bear. For at that time there was no one in the country who did not feel resentment and disgust at the personal conduct and public behaviour of the king. He, on the other hand, wasn't even ashamed when disgusting pimps appeared everywhere with his entourage. He did not confine them within the limits of his frivolous, playboy private life, but even allowed them to interfere effectively in matters of state. Certain of his advisers attempted to alert him to the danger of that course and the evil result of it, but he would not accept the advice. In fact, some of the politicians signed and presented to him a formal but loyal petition requesting him to purge his palace of such members of his entourage. He was angered and paid not attention to them. And everything continued on its familiar course. Thus when I heard the army communiqué, I did not sense that anything dangerous would happen. It was merely a protest like other protests.

So I put my clothes on and went out that morning (Wednesday, 23 July 1952) and headed toward Sulayman Pasha Square to take my usual breakfast. Suddenly, I found in the square two Egyptian army tanks. The affair was, then, to be more serious than I had anticipated. We had been accustomed during the occupation to seeing British army tanks in such places – but our Egyptian army tanks, and especially after a communiqué challenging the king, that was something that had never occurred to us. I went into Groppi's[4] and found some acquaintances there talking about the matter. The conversation warmed up, voices rose, and people known and unknown participated in the debate. I began to realize that dangerous events lay ahead of us. On the next day, Thursday, I left my office in Dar al-Kutub to catch the desert-road[5] bus which left at four o'clock in the afternoon for Alexandria. I went straight to my summer house and didn't leave it until Friday morning. Then I saw army vehicles coming and going all along the Corniche with people applauding enthusiastically. I myself was also very enthusiastic, but there was no one in Egypt who was not enthusiastic about this army which on its own had been able to stand against that king, who was universally disliked for his sordid character and for his body which was so bloated that he looked like a pig.

It was as though fate had willed his end and had blinded him to the path that would have saved him. The first signs of the storm had already appeared. The king had confronted them by the formation of a weak and implausible new ministry. He had appointed as minister of defence the gentle young Isma'il Shirin,[6] who was the husband of the king's sister, Fawziyah, but even Isma'il immediately understood that the situation had become more dangerous and the responsibility greater than the likes of him or of that ministry could bear. He had hardly sworn the oath of allegiance to the king when he got down on his knees and begged the king by right of their relationship to listen to the truth, namely, that he should bring in as prime minister the one man who could confront the situation and save the throne – the leader of the majority, Mustafa al-Nahhas Pasha.[7] Al-Nahhas had continued to maintain a broad spectrum of popularity in the country. His appearance at that moment would have won the masses over to his side, and they would then have inclined to him and to the solution which he favoured. In any case, he was a man who was known to act within the limits of the constitution.

THE KING'S HESITATION

But the king hesitated. Perhaps it was too difficult for him to go to his traditional enemy for a way out of his impasse. In response to the insistence of his youthful relative, he turned the matter over to his *chef du cabinet*, Dr Hafiz 'Afifi,[8] an enemy of al-Nahhas and his party. 'Afifi's opinion was of course known, and thus the king lost his chance. Affairs moved forward at a startling pace. On my way back to Cairo on the desert bus on Saturday afternoon, 26 July 1952, we stopped at the drive-in called The Rest House, and I ordered a cup of coffee. The voice of the broadcaster on the radio in the place was announcing the news of the king's departure from the country following his abdication. There is no question about it, the feeling of happiness in the country was genuine.

THE NEW MASTERS

The country looked the new masters over. Who were they? No one knew anything about them except that their chief, who was cited in the name of the movement by the communiqués which were published in the papers and broadcast over the radio, was a major-general in the army named Muhammad Najib. His name had been heard in recent months because, it was said, army men and especially the younger officers had presented him as a candidate for the presidency of the officers' club – a candidacy which the king had opposed. The king eliminated him and put forward one of his protégés. But General Najib had remained the darling of the young officers and then appeared at their head in this movement which led to the expulsion of the king.

Now, the situation having stabilized and everything being in the hands of the movement's leaders, what were they going to do? According to what I heard, it was General Muhammad Najib's opinion that the army should not rule, should leave ruling to the people in a constitutional way, and should return to its barracks and oversee the course of events from nearby. It is said that he was in contact with the leader of the majority party, Mustafa al-Nahhas, on this score and that telephone conversations between them had been heard. Then dissension broke out between the commanding general and his colleagues, the young officers.

THE OFFICERS AND PYGMALION

At that time one of my friends, a brilliant journalist in close contact with those young officers, reported to me: "They say that the affair is like your play 'Pygmalion'."[9] What they meant was that it was the officers who had turned Muhammad Najib into a statue which was being presented to the people as though he were the leader of the movement, whereas in fact they themselves had initiated it. They had planned it, written broadsides on its behalf in the name of the "free officers", and had set the deadline for executing the plan. But they had kept a low profile before the people because they were young and of low military rank. They were afraid the people would not take seriously a movement undertaken by a group of obscure, inexperienced junior officers. They absolutely had to have a mature face, of at least the rank of major-general, to put in the vanguard from behind which they would lead. They chose Major-General Muhammad Najib and set him up as a statue based on the movement. But now he had become well established in the eyes of the people, had forgotten that he was only a statue, and had begun to give his opinion freely on the political future of the country. Thus they thought of the statue of Pygmalion. But I wondered whether any one of them had really read my play or whether they had merely known and heard of the name and the title? Whatever the case, in my play Pygmalion threw his statue down after a while, and this is exactly what the officers did with their statue.

But the question remains: did they plan from the beginning to get rid of Muhammad Najib as soon as he had completed his task? Or did events force them to do it? Some say that certain generals and politicians advised Muhammad Najib to proceed immediately to get rid of those young visionaries, but that they were quicker than he and lunched on him before he was able to dine on them. It was also said –

and I don't know whether it is a fact or a rumour – that the Sudan strongly supported Muhammad Najib and his leadership. His mother was Sudanese, and the Sudanese were prepared to unite their country with Egypt under the leadership of Muhammad Najib. Had this process been completed, it would have meant the final consolidation of Najib's power and the end of any thought of dismissing or getting rid of him. Thus, so it was said – and the responsibility for its truth rests with those who did the saying – the "free officers" quickly dispatched someone to the Sudan to sabotage this possibility.

PARTY DISPUTES

No doubt history must one day subject all these rumours or facts to minute scrutiny. . . .

There is another question. Did these "free officers" plan to rule the country themselves, or did circumstances in the country at the time push them relentlessly into it? I of course cannot know their inner intentions, but by direct observation I do know, as many knew at the time, what the situation in the country was in so far as party disputes and moral opportunism were concerned. One among many of these party disputes which I myself became aware of is as follows: the revolution had taken place, and its successive events summoned me to adhere to it. I used to pass by the newspaper *Akhbar al-Yawm*[10] every evening to find out what was going on. One evening I found there my old journalist friend, the late Tawfiq Diyab,[11] owner of the Wafdist paper, *Al-Jihad.*[12] We had hardly seated ourselves before one of the senior men of the Liberal Constitutional Party, which opposed the Wafd,[13] came in on us, namely the late Ahmad 'Abd al-Ghaffar Pasha.[14] Lo and behold, these two fell all over each other with hugs and kisses and exchanged the most delicate expressions of loving welcome. Then they began to speak about the new situation, the fate of the constitution, and the need for all political parties to take a single stance and put an end to disagreements, and for every politician to extend his hand to the other in order that their position be unified – all with the purpose of preserving the constitution of the country. Ahmad 'Abd al-Ghaffar said, "Who will guarantee your good intentions, Wafd party?" Tawfiq Diyab answered, "If there were to be treachery, well, you were always the masters of treachery, you party of the minority." There followed a word from this one and a word from that one, and I did not feel anything except the voices which mounted into curses on both sides: the loud, piercing voice of Ahmad 'Abd al-Ghaffar shouted out, "Who would put his hand in your hands, you Wafdists, you party of rabble, you dogs?" Tawfiq Diyab bellowed back, "Shut up, stupid – you and your miserable party, you stooges of the British . . . ." The matter did not end even with their blasting each other with curses and vilification; in the end it led to blows and punches.

THE TWO POLITICIANS COME TO BLOWS

In fact, 'Abd al-Ghaffar raised his cane to frighten his adversary. Diyab, with all his ample body, rushed forward to strike his enemy. I could not figure out any way to avoid getting involved in separating them. So I grabbed Tawfiq Diyab's jacket in order to push him back. Then his foot slipped, he fell on the ground, and I fell with him. Then he got up, tried to get out of the grip that I had on his jacket, and yelled, "Leave me alone! Lay off! I have to teach him manners and bash his dirty brains in!" 'Abd al-Ghaffar, for his part, kept on brandishing his upraised cane in the air, frothing with rage, and redoubling his curses on Tawfiq and all Wafdists. I found no approach which would enable me to get my friend outside. When I did succeed in getting him out, I advised him to go home immediately and lie down. I knew that he had recently suffered a heart attack, and I was afraid of the effect of this "conversation" on his health. Then I returned to Ahmad 'Abd al-Ghaffar to try to calm him down, but it was no use. It became absolutely clear to me that night that nothing could cure the illness of partisanship and party fanaticism in this country.

A REVOLUTION AGAINST THE CONSTITUTION

But what happened to the constitution in force in Egypt at that time? I was given the following account. After the success of the officers' movement in expelling King Faruq and extracting from him the abdication document, which Sulayman Hafiz,[15] the vice president of the council of state had personally delivered to him in his palace at al-Muntazah, the "free officers" should have proceeded with those measures specified in the constitution for a regency. Some claimed that the leader of the majority party, al-Nahhas Pasha, had agreed with the officers on all these constitutional measures. They included convening the dissolved chamber of deputies in order to submit to it the names of the regents in conformity with the regulations of the constitution. The chamber would then take the necessary measures for holding new elections. But Sulayman Hafiz, who was also an enemy of the Wafd, frightened the officers out of their wits in this matter. He told them that free elections would certainly result in a Wafdist parliament, and asked what made them think that this parliament would support them. He advised them to disregard the constitution and opined that they had the right to issue laws without any parliament because they had established a revolution. Revolution meant the abrogation of whatever had been established before it. Thus the term *revolution* came to be applied to the movement of 23 July although it had previously been called *movement*. Because of our love for it, it had even been dubbed *blessed movement*. Certain university professors now also began to assert the term *revolution* and to support the officers' absolute right to issue laws.

THE MOVEMENT BECOMES A REVOLUTION

From another angle, however, some who were specialists in constitutional law undertook to deny to the movement the title of *revolution*. They argued that the term which should be applied to the movement was *military overthrow*. A revolution, they argued, has to have been carried out by the people and led by civilians as was the case of the French revolution, which had been brought about by the people and led by civilians; of the Russian revolution, which had been brought about by the people under the leadership of Lenin; and of the Egyptian revolution of 1919, which the people had brought about under the leadership of civilians. A movement brought about by an armed group of military men was an "overthrow of the system of rule". The "free officers" of course did not accept the second opinion. They grew distant to its adherents, welcomed the first viewpoint, and drew closer to those who advocated it. Thus the movement became a revolution, and there came to be a council of the revolution which issued laws in closed rooms without any opposition and without any public debate.

WHERE WERE WE? . . .

But where were *we*? Where were the thinkers in this country? And where was I who loved freedom of thought? The fact is that we – and to the fullest extent of the word I mean myself and my feelings – felt no constraint. On the contrary, I was happy with the coming of these young men and dazzled by what they had undertaken in throwing out the king. No one had imagined that it could have been done with such ease. At that time we, of course, did not pay sufficient attention to the grievousness of the loss of our constitutional life. Why? Because we were emerging from a stage in which the constitution had lost its sanctity and in which democracy had greatly degraded the constitution and had made of it a vehicle for opportunists and a short cut for *les ministrables*. I had written about this point in my book *Shajarat al-Hukm*,[16] in which I had expressed my opinion, which I had broadcast in 1938, that the parliamentary system as it was being applied in Egypt was the soundest means for producing unsound rulers and that parliament in the true sense had ceased to oversee the actions of the government. I further argued that home and school had the responsibility to increase the inculcation of high ideals among the young and also to persuade the young that they were the ones to reform one day all this corruption and thus to bring about a "blessed revolution" which would inspire the fatherland to a state of soundness, strength and order. I wrote these exact expressions long years before the revolution of 1952.[17] Thus there should be no surprise that I welcomed this revolution and did not grieve for the loss of the constitution. This then is my responsibility, and if the constitution had been lost on the advice of men of rancour and prejudice, it was not the first time. For previously, on the day that Faruq ascended the throne and as an innocent young fellow undertook his constitutional powers, the constitution had been desecrated on similar advice. It had not occurred to him that the constitution of the country could be desecrated, but some of his consultants and advisers – those of the palace men who were close to him like 'Ali Mahir[18] and Ahmad Hasanayn[19] – wanted to convert him from a constitutional monarch into an absolute ruler so that they themselves could rule behind his façade. They taught him that he was above the constitution and that he should seize the first opportunity to indicate to the people that he was *the* strong ruler. They chose as the right opportunity for him the day al-Nahhas was elected majority leader and came forward with his ministerial slate. They advised the king to refuse some of the nominees and to make substitutions and adjustments in the proposed slate. This violation of the constitution marked the beginning of that period in which all true democratic life was destroyed.

PRINCIPLES WITHOUT PERSONS

Thus it was that the trampling down of our lost constitution was eased for us – and most especially for me. In my view the principles were endowed with no value in the absence of persons who applied them sincerely, who believed in them, and strove for them. The actuality was that we had principles and constitutions in the hands of people who played with them for their own benefit and their own ends while our continual dream and expectation had been the appearance of sincere people. These young officers indicated to us – and most particularly to me – that they had come as sincere men to reform the country. They courageously proclaimed that which we had long been advocating but which we had never before found any one to listen to. They began by abolishing titles. How often had we written and published our ridicule of them. In my book *Taht Shams al-Fikr*[20] there is a chapter entitled "The Clique of Dignitaries" in which I ridiculed titles such as "the possessor of rank",[21] "the possessor of the state",[22] "the possessor of nobility",[23] "the possessor of happiness",[24] "the possessor of power"[25] and others. These titles brought to mind a smile when a man like Churchill, who at that time was shaking the world, bore no title other than *mister*, which was the same title that the driver of his car bore. This view was expressed in that book. It also includes passages in which I advocated the necessity of abolishing the fez and of limiting landholdings. In fact, a member of parliament had presented this demand in the previous parliament, to which of course no one paid any attention. Thus when I heard the news of the determined resolve to limit agricultural holdings, I received it warmly.

AL-SANHURI

I learned of this news one summer morning while sitting in a small café on the corniche at Sidi Bishr.[26] Dr 'Abd al-Razzaq al-Sanhuri[27] approached as though he had come looking for me. He was an old friend – since 1935. I was then director of the department of investigations in the ministry of education while he was a professor in the faculty of law. A common set of ideals and reformist positions developed between us. At that time we both lived in Giza,[28] and we used to walk for an hour in the afternoon on the 'Abbas bridge talking at length. Each of us had in his hand a paper cone of seeds bought from a sidewalk vendor, and we dreamt all sorts of plans. One day he came to me with the concept of a useful plan for moulding the youth and inculcating in their souls high ideals and a spirit of achievement. The best method for achieving this goal would be the formation of a society of university students with whom contact would be possible through his capacity as a university professor. The purpose of the society would be to spread these principles. He asked me to help him in this plan by drawing up the necessary implementation. We began to review the heroes of our history who exemplified the great principles which we wanted to inculcate in our young people – men such as 'Umar ibn al-Khattab,[29] Tariq ibn Ziyad,[30] Rameses II, and the like. Days passed, and then one day when I was sitting in the office of the under-secretary, I suddenly became aware of an unusual commotion. The minister was calling his deputy on the telephone from a cabinet meeting then in progress. The ministry at that time was opposed to the Wafd and Wafdists. The deputy minister was running hither and thither carrying files. I asked him what was going on, and he replied, "The cabinet is meeting in order to fire Dr al-Sanhuri from the university". I was thunderstruck. "Why? What did he do?" He replied, "Dr al-Sanhuri, who is a professor at the university, has formed a university-student political organization to spread propaganda for the Wafd on the advice of his friend al-Nuqrashi Pasha,[31] who is a Wafdist". I could not believe what I had heard, but he re-affirmed it. "What is this nonsense? It is unadulterated slander. This 'organization' is an ethical society designed to spur young people to high ideals and to imitate 'Umar ibn al-Khattab, Tariq ibn Ziyad, and Rameses II." He laughed sarcastically, "Oh, be quiet, Who's 'Umar ibn al-Khattab and who's Rameses II? You don't know anything. The reports of the department of public security in the ministry of interior and of the political police in these papers and dossiers have verified everything".

I swore to him by my honour that al-Sanhuri was being oppressed, that he and I were partners in this worthy and ethical project, and that if al-Sanhuri had to be removed for this reason, then I should be removed with him. He insisted that it was a political matter, that the society had partisan political goals, and that the Wafdist al-Nuqrashi had had a hand in it, that the subject had not been disclosed to me in its true light, and that only the good aspects of it had been disclosed to me. In short, it was nothing more than a purely political operation. I was absolutely stunned. It was not long before the ministry which had fired al-Sanhuri fell and was succeeded by a Wafdist government in which al-Nuqrashi was a minister. He then in fact held his hand out to al-Sanhuri, restored him to office, smoothed the way for him, first to the deanship of the faculty of law and, subsequently, to the post of deputy minister of education. However, none of this affected my personal friendship for al-Sanhuri.

THE BEGINNING OF THE LIMITATION OF LAND OWNERSHIP

When he came that morning to the Sidi Bishr café to ask about me, al-Sanhuri was president of the council of state. The officers of the revolution had confidence in him and frequently consulted him. I asked him what the news was. He said, "Do you want us to sit and talk like this on an important matter in the middle of the street, so to speak, in the likes of this little café? Get up and let's go to some more private garden restaurant. . . ." He took me by the hand and led us to a suitable place. Then he said, "Listen . . . the men of the revolution want to limit agricultural landholdings, and we now have before us two suggestions: one is to place the absolute limit on ownership at 500 feddans,[32] the other is to make it 200." I wouldn't let him finish what he was saying and bawled out at him, "200 . . . 200 . . . make it 200!" We were ardent in the extreme because of the length of what we Egyptians had endured by way of hesitation, refusal and postponement. I always remember that moment, and I have often repeated it to some of our old acquaintances who had owned hundreds of acres of land. And whenever they cursed, in front of me, this revolution which took away their lands, I insisted to them that the revolution was being wronged. Yes, we were ardent about those moves, and happy at the revolution's response to the feelings and the demands which had previously preoccupied us.

ABOUT THE ABOLITION OF THE FEZ

Yes, we saw that many of our demands and wishes were coming to pass quickly and easily at a time when the slightest and most trivial thing for which we had asked in the past had been derailed by obstructions and then evaporated in disputations. The simplest of such changes was removing that symbol of Ottoman dependency, the fez – a headgear which does not give any warmth in the winter or any protection from the sun in the summer. How simple, but no one had succeeded in getting rid of it or changing it. The former journalist, Mahmud ʻAzmi,[33] had wanted to appeal for that step in the 1920s by wearing a hat, but not a soul followed him, and he was forced to take it off and go back to the fez. The eyes of the reformers turned to Saʻd Zaghlul,[34] the leader of the revolution, to take the first step in this cause. If he had taken it, most of the nation would have followed him especially since the leader of the Turkish revolution, Kemal Atatürk had at that time issued a decree abolishing the fez in Turkey. How could the fez cease in the land which had brought it to us while we hung on to it? But Saʻd Zaghlul did not want to undertake movements or reforms that might cause polemics and controversies and thus lead to divisions in the nation at a time when it needed unity and consolidation in order to oppose the British occupation. When the 1930s came, the drive was renewed, and I participated in it. Disputes increased in the pages of the newspapers between me and Khalil Thabit, the managing editor of the conservative paper *Al-Muqattam*.[35] The whole thing ended with me alone taking off the fez and wearing a beret – which I chose because it is very much like our native *taqiyyah*.[36] I kept on with it until one day I saw many berets adorning heads.

THE DISSOLUTION OF THE PARTIES AND THE TRIAL OF THEIR LEADERS

The rapid implementation, immediately after the revolution, of decisions whose implementation had preoccupied us for years and generations dazzled us, and we began unconsciously to march behind this revolution. The revolution[37] felt that it had achieved such a level of success that it had become the repository of the people's confidence and the anchor of their hopes; and it wanted to have firm authority. But the political parties still existed. One day these parties would wake up, get together, and demand a return to constitutional life. But if that were to happen, what would be the position of the army men who had undertaken the movement? At this juncture the revolution began to dissolve all the parties; but that was not enough. There were still polticians of intelligence in the country, men who had big names in almost every field and who were reasonably well considered in various walks of life – names which might, in juxtaposition, diminish the unknown young officers, the mention of whose names did not yet inspire a picture of accumulated experience, knowledge or culture. Here also the revolution came forward with a master stroke, which almost rivalled that of Muhammad 'Ali against the Mamluks in the citadel of Cairo.[38] I refer to the creation of the "revolutionary tribunal". To it came most of the political men who had considerable value and an illustrious name. It stripped them absolutely of their dignity and made them stand before it and before the people naked, weak, frightened and greedy. Everyone of them defamed his colleague in order to save himself or obtain favour with the rulers. The revolutionary officers pointed them out and said to the people, "These are those who used to rule you."

However, a number of these politicians stood up to the tribunal and spoke a word of truth and courage without overloading their language or defaming any colleague. An example, according to what we heard, relates to the politician and littérateur, Dr Muhammad Husayn Haykal.[39] The court asked him "why" he, the leader of a party, had not stood up in the face of the tyranny of Faruq. He replied calmly to the officers of the court, "Because Faruq used to frighten us with you, gentlemen of his army. Was not Faruq the commander-in-chief of the army and were not you his men?" This was, of course, true. What would a civilian political party do against an army? In fact, it was a question which had no place there. But then the likes of this tribunal had not expected from the likes of these politicians in the likes of their humiliating situation such embarrassing answers.

Those important men of Egypt who did not appear before this tribunal were nevertheless called in by the men of the revolution one after another, alone, in order that they also be heard from. Their situation was no different from those in the court. Each competed with the other in currying favour – exalting himself, his opinion, and his advice while putting down others and declaring their opinions foolishness. The preferred game of the new rulers was to beat one with the other and to delight in watching these fine and eminent people grovel on their knees because of fear and avarice in this arena of flattery and cajoling. . . .

THE MOVEMENT OF PURIFICATION

The new rulers followed these procedures up with a major blow which spread its traces throughout the whole country, overturned the scales, and demolished the old regime down to the smallest detail. It was called the "movement of purification". What it amounted to was the incitement of every employee to complain about his chief, every inferior to attack his superior, and every colleague to roast his peer. The various agencies, departments, ministries, universities, hospitals – in fact all types of activity in Egypt – were converted into battlegrounds of truth and falsehood but mostly of falsehood because the defamer in most cases coveted the post of the defamed. In other cases the complainant was a pure agitator by nature to whom an opportunity for trouble making was given. No chief of a department or director of an agency was free from the complaints of those under him, nor was any professor in a university spared from the defamation of a colleague.

A COMPLAINT AGAINST ME

No one was saved from disgrace in this turmoil. Before I, the director of Dar al-Kutub, realized it, a complaint was suddenly lodged against me by an employee who loved to stir up trouble. What can one say given that our work in Dar al-Kutub was not of the type that permits shortcomings, but he found something. In that frantic atmosphere one could no doubt find a complaint about something somewhere, but I had not imagined that useful work would become the source of a complaint. What had I done? The yarn was that on the first day I took over my post at Dar al-Kutub, I had found in my office something that looked like a sofa covered with green broadcloth. I started to sit on it, but the secretary stopped me. Then he pulled off the cover, and, lo and behold, it was an enormous Koran, measuring one metre by two with a pure silver cover. It was said to have been a gift to Dar al-Kutub from an Indian maharaja. I was surprised that it had been placed like that in the office of the director, and I conceived it to be my duty to display the precious masterpiece so that the people could see it. Then I got up to make an inspection tour of the library and found large wooden boxes thrown so negligently that cockroaches could practically live in them. I ordered them opened, and they contained examples of beautiful Persian miniatures of the seventeenth century which depicted scenes from the *Thousand and One Nights*, *Kalilah wa-Dimnah*,[40] and the like. Again I was surprised, and I said, "Better the masses view 'em than let the roaches chew 'em." Then I was visited by the Austrian scholar Grohmann,[41] who is a specialist known internationally for his books and researches on the documents relating to the Islamic papyri. I was able to get from him for the library exquisite examples of papyrus manuscripts which disclose the nature of private, public and commerical transactions in Islamic Egypt from the time of 'Amr ibn al-'As.[42]

At the time I thought that I might display all these rare treasures in a kind of museum-like exhibit which they who were dubious about Dar al-Kutub could view. It happened that at that time there was visiting Cairo a French lady who worked for the Louvre in Paris and who was the niece of M. Drioton,[43] the director of the Egyptian Museum and a specialist in Egyptian antiquities. He was a friend of mine, and I had asked him to permit me to invite his niece to assist me in organizing that exhibit. She placed the great silver Koran, with its pages open, in the middle of the room and screened the perimeter of the room with a red velvet screen supported by slender brass columns. Then she indicated the workmanship of the wooden chests by using glass panels to depict the Persian art and also displayed examples of Islamic papyrus manuscripts. The show was a success. Every day droves of visitors, especially foreign tourists, came to see it. What, you ask, is the crime in this? The complaint stated that I had spent public monies to compensate a foreign lady because she was a relative of one of my foreign friends. The truth is that no money at all was spent on this lady visitor. She had undertaken this service voluntarily out of the goodness of her heart. Of course the charge was dropped, but it is one example among many which led me to conclude that the evil of opening this door is greater than its value. In fact, it led to many oppressive accusations, to the ruination of the reputations of some of the best people, and to the removal of some of the best professors and scholars. However, the most dangerous aspect of it all was the spread of chaos in the administrative system itself. A chief's fear of his subordinates diminishes his authority and the respect in which he is held: the reins are in effect abandoned. If the revolution wanted a situation to evolve so that no important person in the country should have any authority other than the revolution's authority and so that the revolution should strike down the high by using the low, it should also have anticipated that this policy might harm the revolution itself. When the revolution became stabilized and introduced absolute rule in the country, it found itself faced by chiefs and directors in all agencies, departments and sections who had lost the courage to take responsibility.

The "purification" operations proceeded without care or reckoning to the extent that they included some senior officials who were chosen a little later as ministers in the very government which had previously destroyed them for purposes of "purification". By way of example, I cite Engineer 'Abd al-Malik Sa'd,[44] the former minister of communications, and Dr 'Abd al-Razzaq Sidqi,[45] the previous minister of agriculture.

MY ENTHUSIASM FOR THE "BLESSED MOVEMENT"

But that the degree of danger in this situation merited criticism had not yet become apparent to us. Revolutions imply many mistakes, and we tolerate them; in fact, we seldom pay attention to them or even consider them mistakes. But when revolutions eventuate in momentous, earth-shaking disasters which undermine the fate of the nation, then these mistakes are exposed to view and require investigation. It is like a flourishing tree whose trunk harbours woodworms. No one pays any attention to the woodworms as long as the tree stands and is fruitful. But if it should fall over or its leaves turn yellow, then people would investigate the disease, and everybody would pay attention to what woodworm had infested it.

At the time we did not pay any attention to the results because the results had not yet appeared. We were in the midst of a revolution which every day issued rapid-fire decrees beneficial to the people. They all evidenced good intention toward reform. I still remember perfectly all my feelings toward it. I never for a moment felt anything except absolute enthusiasm for the measures it took even when spillover from the downpour of complaints about "purification" ended up affecting me. It had been my opinion – a view that had appeared often in my writings before the revolution – that Egypt had been stricken under the rule of Faruq with the maladies of party factionalism, self-interest and social oppression. Thus we used to long for change. In fact, in my book *Shajarat al-Hukm* I used some strange expressions, which now have the ring of prophecy, about the necessity of undertaking, I quote literally, " a blessed movement and a blessed revolution".[46] Later, when it actually came, it was given this name from its very first appearance.

. . . All these points affirm beyond any doubt my spiritual commitment to the essence of the revolution and my belief that it constituted the realization of my hopes and my point of view. As the poem says,

> The happy eye obscures every sin
> As the bitter eye sees every fault within.

I, then, have never been one of those people who were embittered against the revolution which I had predicted and awaited. I wanted to protect it and to overlook its sins in the hope that those sins would cure themselves with the passage of time.

WHEN THE MINISTER WANTED TO FIRE ME

The revolution proceeded on its course: success was its ally, and the people's applause focused on it. Its first ministry even included some civilians. The revolution appointed to the ministry of education, to which Dar al-Kutub was attached, a minister who had been one of the important educators in the previous regime and who was a friend of mine. It happened at that time that one of my plays had been translated into German and produced in Salzburg in the Mozarteum theatre, named after the composer Mozart. I was invited to attend and I went. It was a serious cultural celebration during which the provincial governor gave a big lunch in my honour. In it they praised me most generously. The Egyptian ambassador described it in a report, accompanied by articles from German newspapers, which he sent to the ministry of foreign affairs. When I returned to Egypt, I found that my friend, the minister of education had presented to the council of ministers a request to terminate my employment in accordance with the decree on "purification". The grounds were that I was an unproductive employee. I knew nothing about this action which was all taken behind my back. Apparently, some of those who coveted my post had instigated the minister to take this step. Later, I learned what had happened. The minister had been challenged by one of the leaders of the revolution. In fact, he was challenged by the ablest one of them, the one with the strongest personality, and the one whose name had begun to shine out among them, Jamal 'Abd al-Nasir. As I heard it, he shouted at the civilian minister, "Do you want us to kick out a writer who is returning from a European country showered with praise? Do you want them to say that we are ignorant?" The end of the affair was the expulsion of the minister from his post. . . .

It was undoubtedly a good omen that circumstances had at that time brought about this revolution, for it appeared that, as a result, a young army officer conducted himself better, valued cultured people more highly, and understood culture more than a senior educational official of mature age from the previous regime. . . !

I DID NOT MEET 'ABD AL-NASIR

'Abd al-Nasir began to refer to this affair frequently in conversations with journalists and foreign correspondents: "I fired a minister for the sake of an intellectual." Nevertheless, it did not occur to me to thank him either face to face or in writing, and I don't know why. . . ? Possibly it was because the practice of maintaining a certain distance from the politically powerful had taken root in my soul despite the fact that well-known individuals in the country, in every field, had hastened to seek meetings with the ruling army men. Indeed, I remember that a star journalist friend of 'Abd al-Nasir visited me one day in my Dar al-Kutub office and informed me that the head of the government, Jamal 'Abd al-Nasir, was inviting me to have tea in his house. It was to be a special invitation attended only by me. I said to him apologetically, "How can I go to the head of the government when I am only a government employee of under-secretarial rank? My contacts are with the deputy minister or by the farthest stretch with my own minister." He laughed and said, "He is not inviting you in your capacity as a government employee but as the author of *'Awdat al-Ruh*,[47] which he has read and which he says has influenced the formation of his nationalism." I said to him, "Even so, I beg you to keep some distance between me and the rulers." After that, whenever he saw me, he said to those present, "Here is the man who refused to meet 'Abd al-Nasir." I would try to lighten the situation, "Not the person of 'Abd al-Nasir but the ruler. I have never in my life met the head of a government while he was in power." He would laugh and say, "What you want is for him to resign in order to see you." I would smilingly reply that, "Yes, indeed, that was the solution."

DISTANCE FROM POWER

'Abd al-Nasir was, apparently, astonished at my keeping my distance from him. I heard that he made such remarks as, "Have we not done that about which he thought, felt, and wrote? The revolution is really his revolution." The fact is that his view was reasonable and logical. What kept me away was my well-known principle about which I had often written: a ruler does not want free thought from a thinker; what he wants is "kept" thought. In fact what he really wants to hear from him is support not opposition. On the other hand, the mission of the thinker is in its essence truth and freedom. He may err, go astray, and lose consciousness, but he should never consciously betray his mission. I have always feared that friendship, kinship, love and affection, and indeed dislike and anger, conceal a truthful look at the realities of things. In my *Sijn al-'Umr*[48] I tried as much as possible to portray the people closest to me – my parents – with both their good and bad qualities and without that sanctification which people in our country are accustomed to employ in regard to their own relatives. Thus I risked the anger of my living relatives and the condemnation of conservative readers. . . .

THE ABSOLUTE RULER

Things went along their way. 'Abd al-Nasir became the first man in the country. Every day he acquired greater love and confidence from the people. Even many of those whose estates had been taken over for the purpose of the land reform began to become accustomed and acclimatized to the limitation of ownership, although there were some for whose loyalty there was no hope. The country began to become accustomed to one-man rule, to have confidence in it, and to like it. And when the masses like something, they do not debate. Little by little the voices of those who *were* accustomed to debate died down, and the beloved ruler himself began to become accustomed to rule without debate. The iron curtain was gradually lowered between the people and the conduct of the absolute ruler. We loved him without knowing the inner springs of his thought or the true motivation for his conduct. Our heart penetrated the curtain to reach him, but the mind remained separated from him. It arrived at no understanding of what was going on behind the veil. We only knew of our own affairs, or of external affairs, or what he tossed down to us from his lofty podium on some formal holiday or other occasion. For long hours he used to deliver by himself, without any formality, a speech in which he pictured his leadership in heroic proportions while describing the major powers around us as though they were dwarfs. We would clap in proud surprise. When he delivered a powerful speech and said about a strong country which had the atomic bomb that "If they don't like our conduct, let them drink from the sea", he filled us with pride.

CONFIDENCE PARALYSES THOUGHT

What is not surprising is that the people, in the heat of their affection, received these speeches with jubilation[49] and glorification.[49] What *is* surprising is that an intellectual like me, accountable to his country, whom the revolution overtook while he was fully mature, could also be pulled along behind this affectionate heat. It did not occur to me to think about the truth of the picture which was being manufactured for us . . .; perhaps I justified the lapse to myself on the grounds that the revolution was trying to raise the morale of the people. In fact, there is no obvious harm as long as the evil results continue to be remote. . . . Confidence apparently had paralysed thought. From time to time I used to think that something that happened was odd, and I would say to myself, "Is this thing which happened right?" I remember one day when a brilliant journalist friend, and a friend of 'Abd al-Nasir, brought me a copy of 'Abd al-Nasir's book *The Philosophy of the Revolution*,[50] dedicated to me by its author, our leader. After I read it, I thought: "How can it be right for a politician to show his cards to the whole world?"

ISRAEL DISTRIBUTES *THE PHILOSOPHY OF THE REVOLUTION*

Later, I happened to see an article in a French newspaper by a French professor of history and politics. He analysed the book scientifically and described its content of dreams, hopes and fantasies which all added up more or less to a desire to create something like a vast empire composed of Arab and African states who were, presumably, waiting for the leader who would form it. According to the book itself, alluding to Pirandello's famous play *Six Characters in Search of an Author*, he was aiming at "nationalistic Arab states and others in search of a leader".[51] Later I was astonished at an item that appeared in some internationally known newspapers to the effect that two quarters had assumed responsibility for the foreign distribution of this book, *The Philosophy of the Revolution*: the Egyptian embassy and the Israeli embassy.

Of course the aim of the last-mentioned embassy was to make the world understand that a leader of the Hitler type had appeared in the Arab world . . . , but the truth is that 'Abd al-Nasir was a man of peace. He never thought an effective thought about war. He was a man of feeling, of excitation and agitation, of imagination. In fact, a passage appears in the book of the brilliant journalist Muhammad Hasanayn Haykal,[52] to the effect that 'Abd al-Nasir, at the beginning of his administration, had prepared a speech in which he announced some step toward, or at least a dream of, peace in the region. However, before he had delivered the speech, he heard from the then American ambassador some remarks, with which the ambassador had greeted the president during a visit, that he had not liked. 'Abd al-Nasir became agitated and immediately changed his speech and his course. This agitated conduct had an effect on the whole destiny of Egypt since thereafter all state matters, external and internal, proceeded on this basis. The motor force was: "excitation and reaction".

EXCITATION AND REACTION

A person who carefully studies the political, military and social events that took place in Egypt throughout the rule of 'Abd al-Nasir will find that their true unseen motor force was "excitation and reaction", and not calm, composed and serious thought built up on the basis of a long-term veiw of things. From mistakes whose results we still reap, it appears that 'Abd al-Nasir was not a political man and in no way had the natural qualities of a man of politics such as those possessed by other leaders whom he knew, men such as Nehru and Tito. It is known that, in a neat and inspired phrase, Nehru said of 'Abd al-Nasir that he needed a little white hair. What he no doubt meant was a little composure, wisdom and experience, and it later appeared that Nehru was right. 'Abd al-Nasir was unable to achieve impartiality as his two real heroes, Nehru and Tito, could. They were true politicians. 'Abd al-Nasir had more of the nature of a dreamy, emotional, artistic writer. It appears that circumstances had driven him into a path other than his own. Left to his own nature, he would have been a successful writer. Perhaps this idea is what came to him at the beginning, for he in fact inclined in his early youth to storywriting. He wrote pages of a story entitled "On the Road to Freedom", the hero of which was named Muhsin like the hero of my *'Awdat al-Ruh*. But circumstances converted 'Abd al-Nasir, the creator of a Muhsin on paper, into Muhsin himself in life on this earth. He lived like Muhsin and conducted himself in Muhsin's personal, nationalistic, emotional and agitational way even in matters far removed from politics and matters of state. Thus he revealed his emotional and agitational nature.

HE BECOMES AGITATED OVER ME

One day, several of the young writers attacked me with the aim of pulling down idols, and articles began to appear every morning full of charges desiged to sweep this writer away and to remove him from his place. I did not take the matter seriously or pay any attention to it but stayed calm and silent. Suddenly, it was 'Abd al-Nasir who became agitated. Immediately, at the moment of his agitation and on the spur of his reaction, he issued a decree granting me the highest decoration in the state. The major ceremonies connected with it reiterated that this decoration was only awarded to heads of state and heirs apparent. I, a civil servant with the rank of under-secretary, had no right to wear this kind of decoration. In his remarks he did not deny it.

In fact we loved this emotional impetuosity in 'Abd al-Nasir because we had lived for a long time in the past with rulers who were cautious, hesitant and cold, and who would not take a step until the spirit moved them. How much we had suffered from that inaction. So if a fiery, emotional ruler, who stepped fast and daringly, appeared, it was a new phenomenon for us. The ruinous consequences of 'Abd al-Nasir's impetuosity had not yet appeared, and in fact there was in it something that warmed and ignited us by contagion as a result of the onslaught of agitation and the spirit of activity.

CONTACT AT A DISTANCE

And I, especially, . . . how could I not like a man who liked me and stood beside me everywhere, without my looking at him, or directing a word to him, or thanking him? I was in contact with him only at a distance and on certain national positions to which I felt it my duty to call his attention or towards which to encourage him. Take the day on which a preliminary committee of influential people had gathered to prepare for the convening of the national assembly. I was sick in my room watching the sessions of this preliminary committee on television. As I remember, it was chaired by Anwar al-Sadat, but Jamal 'Abd al-Nasir was also present and participating in the discussions. The spirit of freedom in these discussions startled me. At times arguments flared up between some of the members and Jamal 'Abd al-Nasir, the president of the republic, about the understanding of democracy. In those fiery debates 'Abd al-Nasir appeared to be broadminded and patient. He presented his opinion and his commentary and met the national opposition argument for argument without annoyance or irritation until the various points of view were clarified. My hope for the direction of rule in Egypt – the sound direction – was great.

Sound rule in my view could never be dictatorship. My book *Shajarat al-Hukm*, in which I called for and predicted the blessed revolution, contains the following passage:

> However, my criticism of the representational system does not mean that I call for its abolition, for the disappearance of this system from the world in which we live would leave the field to insoluble difficulties. . . . Election, whatever its fault, is the inescapable way as long as people have opinions about the appointment of their rulers.[53]

Thus I couldn't restrain myself from sending a telegram in which I said to him that, while on my sickbed, I had seen a new vision for Egypt taking form before me. He responded to me with a telegram thanking me and wishing me good health. In due course the national assembly met. Debate was stifled. The members who had been discussing matters with the required democracy were forced into a silence imposed not alone in the assembly, but in all public life. It was as though some dereliction of duty or dissatisfaction had permeated them. The assembly and other meetings became mere human lumps undistinguished by intelligence or thought and from which no independent view issued. They were only arms which waved, hands which clapped, and mouths which cheered while the leader, with his tall stature looking down from a lofty dais, spoke alone for long hours uninterrupted except by the hysterical chant, "Nasir! Nasir! Nasir!" and by slogans which burst forth from every corner so that it was impossible to imagine that anyone present could have understood amidst such a din anything that he said. Throats indeed became brains. Apparently the impoverishment of that scene did not occur to the leader, for a satisfied smile was always visible on his lips.

THE IDOLIZED ONE BECOMES INFALLIBLE

He ended up being idolized by the people. I do not know whether or not this eventuality had been an old dream of his, but once I became certain over the course of time that this process of idolization was going on, I began to wonder what had pleased him in my *'Awdat al-Ruh*. Could it have been the paragraph which indicates that Egypt always needs someone of its own to idolize? When as a young fellow he read that, did he dream that one day he would be the one who would be idolized? Such a dream is not wrong, for everyone has the right to dream that he will be idolized by the masses. What *is* wrong, even dangerous, is for the human being who is idolized to acquire such sanctity as to make him infallible in the people's eyes and to make his power paralyse the mind so that the people see nothing except what he sees and be permitted no view contrary to his view. But this is what in fact happened. For the first time in the modern history of Egypt we saw things evolving on this model.

The Egyptian mind, which had been sealed by seven seals, was not prepared to risk coming out publicly with an opinion contrary to the opinion of the idolized leader. Long years passed, and although it was said that 'Abd al-Nasir was the highest authority in the country, Egypt also had a press, a parliament and a socialist union (that single party which embraced all elements of the people). One may well ask, did he hear any single voice in the pages of the newspapers or of a book, or in a parliament, or in a public meeting which dared to express an opinion which differed from the opinion of 'Abd al-Nasir? And if someone had dared, would he have had the power to convey his opposition so that other people would hear it and know of it? I repeat that this was perhaps the first time in the modern history of Egypt in which it happened that an idolized person had appeared who wanted his will to have, throughout the Arab countries, a degree of holiness, greatness and power which not even God's prophets and messengers possessed. Those prophets who were sent from heaven in fact found people who contested their messages, argued against them, and opposed them.

SA'D WAS IDOLIZED BUT FREE

Egypt had known in its recent history one other idolized leader, Sa'd Zaghlul, the leader of the revolution of 1919. Egypt in its entirety revolved around him and placed its hope in him. He became a legend among the fellaheen to the extent that at the time I heard people in the countryside who asserted that certain leaves on cotton plants sprouted and turned green with the name Sa'd Zaghlul written on them. However, the fact that Sa'd's person was worshipped did not preclude the existence of opponents who differed from his opinion, or of papers and speeches which were filled with views and statements that opposed him and stood against him. In fact an opposition paper went so far as to defame him while he was majority leader and head of the government. He went to court and the case was heard, but the just Egyptian judiciary found against the head of government and judged the defendant innocent.

Personally, in spite of my love for Sa'd Zaghlul and my desire to hear him when he delivered speeches from the balcony of his house, a house which was called "the house of the nation", I was strongly opposed to his opinion on one question. At that time there were disagreements on the question of who should go to London to negotiate with the British on the question of the independence of Egypt. At the time [1921] the prime minister was 'Adli Yakan,[54] a trustworthy and upright man. The British government requested that the Egyptian negotiator have an official character, such as the head of the Egyptian government, because the British side would also have an official character. Sa'd Zaghlul insisted, however, that he should be the negotiator because of his informal status as "leader of the nation". Great Britain, which had emerged victorious from the First World War and whose influence in the world was then like that of the United States and the Soviet Union combined, insisted. Its decisive argument was that governments only negotiate with governments and that it was not possible for a responsible government to negotiate with a revolutionary leader who was not officially responsible even if he were in fact the "leader of a nation".

Sa'd Zaghlul delivered his famous speech in which he described the negotiation of 'Adli Yakan, the head of the Egyptian government, with the then government of His Majesty King George as "George the Fifth will negotiate with George the Fifth". The whole thing became so complicated that political initiative concerning the demand for independence almost ceased. One view was: What harm would it do to Sa'd Zaghlul if he allows 'Adli Yakan to go and negotiate and bring back the results of his negotiation and lay them before the nation under the leadership of Sa'd Zaghlul? Sa'd could then either refuse or accept them. This was also what 'Adli Yakan wanted. He saw this scenario as strengthening his position in the negotiation because he would be able to frighten the British with the lurking, waiting Sa'd, who would then have the last word at the end of the affair. This was the procedure that the leader of the Turkish nation Kemal Atatürk had followed, for at exactly that same time Turkey had to send a delegation to negotiate at the peace conference. Mustafa Kemal did not go himself, but left Ismet Inönü to go and negotiate. Whenever some proposal was laid before him, Inönü would exclaim, "Mustafa Kemal, and the nation with him, will never accept this." This point of view appealed to me. I did not support the view of Sa'd Zaghlul even though I was at the beginning of my manhood and despite my love for him and my admiration for his eloquent oratory. This leadership and that idolization were based on free opinion, not on tanks and concentration camps. It is strange that the understanding of free opinion had lasted in Egypt in some form or other even in the periods in which corruption had begun to creep in. In fact, it happened that Mustafa al-Nahhas came to power as a result of elections which he won by a majority. I was at that time director of the department of information in the ministry of social affairs, and I published an article in *Al-Ahram*[55] entitled "The Three Counterfeit Seals" in which I indicated that all the existing parties in the country were counterfeit.

AND MUSTAFA AL-NAHHAS

Mustafa al-Nahhas, being prime minister, got excited: "He says that we are counterfeit although we won the confidence of the nation and received an overwhelming majority." That was all that happened, and no harm came to me even though I was a state employee and the director of information in the government. Among the director's duties was at a minimum the understanding that he be a guide and advocate for his government, not one who attacks it and accuses it of being counterfeit. In their eyes, however, I was above all a free writer expressing a personal opinion and not someone induced by another party to act on its account. Thus they tolerated free expression even when it made life difficult for them.

Moreover, we have seen the idea of an idolized leader whose worship did not exclude his being criticized in France during the era of Charles de Gaulle. Despite the fact that the French sanctified him as a national hero, the existence of those who opposed his views in parliament, in the press, and in books was not forbidden. He, also, was the first to laugh at the caricatures of himself and at the jokes and criticisms with which some of the magazines ridiculed him. The journal which attacked him and his policies, both domestic and foreign, most harshly was the magazine *L'Exprès*.[56] Its chief political editor, Servan-Schreiber,[56] stubbornly opposed the views of de Gaulle in his writings; in the same magazine the novelist François Mauriac would rebut Servan-Schreiber and defend his friend, de Gaulle, who bestowed on him the highest decoration in France. Thus, several years ago, when Sartre visited Egypt, he asked me why I did not also defend 'Abd al-Nasir and write a book in his praise as Mauriac had done in his well-known book on de Gaulle. I said, "For there to be a defence there must be an attack and here no one attacks 'Abd al-Nasir. Nor does anyone in our country dare oppose his view."

In truth, if someone had dared to attack 'Abd al-Nasir's view, how would the author of this dissidence publish his view? In what newspaper? In what place? The censors of the press and of broadcasting, the secret police, and the other organs of the closed absolute order would not have permitted the appearance of opposition, even of the knowledge of a dissident opinion or of its author. In fact, even the concept of opposition would have been immediately distorted and would link its author to treason, deviation, selling out to foreigners, or destructive beliefs.

MAGIC AND DREAMS

The following question may be posed. Had it become clear in an open and serious way by that time that 'Abd al-Nasir had views whose danger and harm necessitated our opposition? Perhaps such things were present, but they appeared to us to be matters which could be overlooked for the sake of the benefit anticipated from him. The truth is that until that time he had inundated us with magic and dreams in such a way that we didn't know how he had inundated us. Perhaps as they said it was his personal magic when he spoke to the masses, or perhaps it was the dream in which we had begun to live because of those hopes and promises. Whatever the fact, those glowing images of the accomplishments of the revolution made out of us instruments of the broad propaganda apparatus with its drums, its horns, its odes, its songs and its films. We saw ourselves as a major industrial state, a leader of the developing world in agricultural reform, and the strongest striking force in the Middle East. The face of the idolized leader, which filled the television screen and loomed at us from the podia of pavilions and of auditoria, related these tales to us for long hours and explained to us how we had been before and what we had now become. No one argued, checked, verified or commented. We could not help but believe, and burn our hands with applause.

THE ORGANIZATION OF APPLAUSE AND CHEERS

The system was not content with spontaneous applause and extemporaneous cheers; rather, its fundamental reliance was on planning and organization. I saw it for myself and I did not believe my eyes. One day I met a man that I knew from the countryside, and I asked him why he was in Cairo. He reported that he was connected with the committee of the Arab Socialist Union[57] in his village and that they had brought him and his colleagues by train in order to create a crowd for the reception of President Jamal 'Abd al-Nasir on his return from abroad. The reception was to be "popular" as they used to say. The participants' lodging and food were at the expense of the state. He and his colleagues' obligation was to cheer the president in accordance with slogans printed and distributed to them. He actually brought out of his pocket for me a piece of paper which he showed me. I was astonished. The following was written on it in printed letters: "Cheer in unison: 'Nasir, Nasir, Nasir.' Cheer by section, 'Long live the victor[58] of Arabism.' Unison: 'Long live the hero of the revolution . . . the leader of the Arab nation'", etc., along these lines. I asked, "How do they cheer from this paper?" He replied that the paper would not appear but was only to memorize from "so that we will not forget the words".

In addition there was an aide who assigned to each group of them ribbons, in the front row or in the middle, or for larger groups and who would point the beginning out to them as happens in a chorale or a chorus.

I used to think that popularity only welled up from the heart or perhaps from the representation of hopes, promises, fancies and lies, but I did not realize until that moment that it could also be manufactured, made up from start to finish, and distributed with paper instructions for cheering like musical notes for singing.

Despite all that – and here is the strange thing – how could a person like me have seen and heard all that without being greatly affected by what he had seen and heard and yet continue to have good feelings toward 'Abd al-Nasir? Had he lost consciousness? Was it a strange case of anaesthetization?

This strange case which afflicted us must one day be the subject of study and investigation. I understand that the feeling should have been repugnance or anger, and at that time, especially for a person like myself, I should have expressed myself on the subject by some form of conduct or in writing no matter what the outcome might have been, as I had previously done on many occasions. The strange thing is that I was content to smile tolerantly . . . why? Perhaps it was because of the hope I had placed in 'Abd al-Nasir – a hope which was the product of my imagination. Or perhaps it was because of the ideal of a leader for whom I had waited thirty years as I had earlier written.

THE EVACUATION AGREEMENT

In any case, neither I nor Egypt as a whole had yet felt constrained by any danger. On the contrary, we had easily digested everything by which we might have been constrained, and no trace of it remained in our souls. Rather, we were happily anticipating the morrow like the father who dreams of the brilliant future of his son. Such a father accepts all his son's mistakes in the hope of his success in the examination and spares no effort in humouring every request the son makes while waiting for the promised day. He does not open his eyes until the day his son fails the examination (like the examination of June 1967), and then the father begins to review the mistakes and to account for the deviations. Even after the failure we justified the errors and were forbearant with the failed son in anticipation of the sequel.

Thus our eyes saw only the good things, and our ears delighted only in the single anthem played everywhere, "The Achievements of the Revolution". Indeed, a sufficient reply either to those who were merely malicious or to those who had actually been wronged and who whispered negative doubts about the revolution was that as long as there were no losses, there was in essence an achievement. Whoever, like me, loved the revolution was inclined toward lenient forbearance after certain doubts had been cleared up, and near certainty was the result. Thus, on the day that the revolutionaries signed the document concerning the British evacuation of Egypt, some of the men of the previous parties came to me and showed me the terms of the document. They stated that they were the same terms and conditions which had been presented to Egypt before the revolution and which the parties had altogether refused. Amongst these terms was the condition that the English be permitted to reoccupy Egypt if the region were exposed to the dangers of war. Similarly, the Sudan and the permanence of its linkage to Egypt had always been a fundamental precondition for every Egyptian negotiator of whatever party. In fact, I remember that I had been sitting at a funeral service following the death of someone in the ministry of education some ten years before the revolution. Mustafa al-Nahhas, who was I believe not then in power, came in and began to talk to those who were with him in his loud, high-pitched voice. He said that the rock on which Anglo-Egyptian negotiations over the evacuation of the British always broke was the Sudan and that if we could set the Sudan aside, we would have finished the negotiations about evacuation in the twenties. But no politician in the country would have permitted himself that course; nor would the country have permitted him. Years passed, the revolution came, the Sudan was abandoned, and the document on the evacuation of the British, also conditioning their return, was signed. Why did Egypt have to wait thirty years? This question was just, but I used to respond that as long as we had got rid of the occupation, in whatever way, it was better than perpetual stalemate and constituted a decisive point leading to movement and a start in building the renaissance of Egypt. The revolution had eliminated this abscess from the face of Egypt so that it could devote itself to something more important. Now, at last, the country was moving toward the desired economic growth.

THE HIGH DAM PROJECT

Lo, the revolution told us, here is the High Dam, which will bring bounty and blessing. The project, of course, had existed on the rolls of our previous governments. It appeared that it had been studied but not executed either because of the hugeness of the expense or for other reasons not frankly revealed to us and not debated in an open public way so that people would understand the opposing views on it. But the revolution proclaimed it, and we all believed in it. We never heard from anyone who opposed it except for one leading engineer, Dr 'Abd al-'Aziz Ahmad,[59] who apparently felt the anger of the revolution. He left the country and when, during his absence, he won the competitive state prize for science, for which he had been chosen by the leading scholars – his colleagues and students – in the country, the revolution refused to grant him the prize. The reasons for his opposition to the project are not known in detail because opposing views were not exposed to the risk of publication.

WITHOUT DEBATE

The style of the revolution was not based on the debate of issues as we in Egypt had known it since the days of the revolution of 1919 – or in fact even before. I remember from my earliest youth that the government had wanted to establish a reservoir, perhaps that of Jabal al-Awliya'[60] – I write from memory. The project was debated before us in the presence of the people even though there was no parliament yet. It happened that an Egyptian engineer opposed the project. He announced that he would give a lecture in the Printania Theatre (now the Cairo Palace cinema), and we went. It was on a Friday morning, and the hall was filled with people. The Egyptian engineer began to explain his view with drawings and figures on the blackboard and to rebut and oppose the view of the English engineer, Willcocks.[61] At that time Egypt was under the British occupation, but this did not prevent Egypt from attempting by itself to create a public opinion which listened, debated, distinguished and decided. However, after the revolution of 1952 took place, with heartfelt love and support offered out of our desire for a better future, we never debated any of the projects which it espoused, and perhaps we could not. Perhaps the revolution itself did not want to encourage that in us, and thus it ploughed ahead immediately to seek the execution of the High Dam project. Of course it relied on America in its execution, for it was America that stood close to the revolution when it took place and which quashed the English garrisoning of the Suez Canal. And if not . . . , the British would have come with their tanks and planes and aborted the revolution in half an hour. But it did not take long before relations between the revolution and America became strained for both known and unknown reasons. It has been said by some that even that strain was planned by American policy in order to lead to the expulsion of England and France from the region and thus to turn the canal over to Egypt in return for opening up the Gulf of Akaba to Israel. . . . This development is what in fact transpired in 1956 by a secret agreement between Eisenhower and 'Abd al-Nasir, an agreement which remained hidden until 1967. That is how Dulles, the American secretary of state, intended the statement which angered 'Abd al-Nasir, whose regular excited reaction was as usual anticipated by America. It was also well known in the Soviet Union, for Khruschev one fine day described 'Abd al-Nasir as a hot-headed excitable young man (Muhammad Hasanayn Haykal, *'Abd al-Nasir wa-al-'Alam*,[62] p. 196). In any case, the order was issued to nationalize the canal with provision for the payment of compensation at a time when the end of the canal concession, including its legal return to Egyptian ownership without paying anything, was less than ten years away. Actually Egypt was attacking itself in taking over the canal. It reminded me of my lifelong friend, the late Hilmi Bahjat Badawi,[63] who had been my schoolfriend through the various stages of study even to Paris and who shared quarters with me in an apartment in Giza at the time when he was a professor in the faculty of law and I was a director of the board of supervisors in the ministry of education. When he was appointed minister of commerce and industry after the revolution, having refused to be minister of finance in the government of Husayn Sirri Pasha,[64] he thought of a project to go side by side with the canal after it had been taken over. The project was to lay oil pipelines from Suez to Port Said or Alexandria. The purpose was to spur the Compagnie Universelle du Canal Maritime de Suez to surrender the canal to Egypt speedily and to achieve other economic goals. He had made good progress in studying the project, in preparing for its execution, and in negotiating with the company over the costs, which at that time were not too high. The general picture was encouraging, and 'Abd al-Nasir approved the project. But later he reversed his decision and stopped the project from going ahead. Now, here we are today once again going back to it and thinking of executing it. Hilmi Bahjat Badawi was on a mission in Europe the day the canal was nationalized and was taken by surprise, but when he returned to Egypt, 'Abd al-Nasir appointed him, in consideration of his ability, to be chairman of the canal authority. He was the first chief to participate in its management on the basis of pure competence and continued as such until his appointed time, unhappily, arrived.

THE "UNEXPECTED" TRIPARTITE AGGRESSION

After nationalization all hell broke loose as everyone knows. I was a prime zealot in favour of nationalization. Some came to me and spoke of their fear that nationalization was crazy, that it would be a disaster for the country. I lashed out violently at those who spoke in that way. And when the armies and the aircraft came to Port Said and the tripartite aggression began, I sent 'Abd al-Nasir a telegram in which I said, "Although I am approaching sixty years of age, I am prepared to bear arms." When I was in the revolution of 1952, I worried about my heart; when I was in the 1919 revolution, I worried about my mind – why, I don't know. The Suez Canal had always been the centre of our hopes, and now it was in our hands. The rest didn't matter. Nevertheless, there were flashes of thought which made me wonder about certain things. I had not forgotten the famous Friday sermon in which 'Abd al-Nasir announced that he did not believe that Britain would actually participate with Israel in aggression against Egypt because in his view such an act would expose the British to the wrath of the Arabs. In fact, he said that he had only learned of British participation when he heard the whine of their planes. Even then, he said, he climbed up to the roof of his own house to make sure, himself, of it. I said to myself, Wait a minute – ! How could our head of state be unaware of this matter when I did not for a moment doubt that Britain was serious about war. After all, I had read the dispatches and heard the broadcasts discussing Eden's meetings with his commanders and his issuing of orders alerting the warships in Malta and the air-base in Cyprus. Some of these ships had even made ready and moved with troops in the direction of the Middle East. 'Abd al-Nasir perhaps interpreted all of these moves to be for purposes of bravado, but I took the affair very seriously because I considered it improbable that a serious, responsible government in a country like Britain would prepare armies and ships, mobilize efforts, transport soldiers, and spend the necessary money simply for bravado. The situation hardly called for massive military preparations and, in fact, there was a solution available; but for various reasons Eden, as it appeared from his insistent tone, had decided to exploit the opportunity to restore British influence in the region. Why then did it occur to ʻAbd al-Nasir that when Eden was talking war and making preparations for it in this way, he was doing it all just by way of bravado?

HE PROVOKES WAR

Men sometimes see things, including other people, through their own natures. Could bravado then have been the nature of ʻAbd al-Nasir? If we review the circumstances of the 1967 war, the disposition of all of our armies in Sinai as though on an awesome parade, of all our tanks new and old, and all our soldiers trained and untrained in order to impress the enemy, to exaggerate in appearance, and to terrorize by effect without there being a true intention of attacking, we find the real intention was to reach the goal by bravado and not by any actual deed. This explanation confirms what I believe, namely, that ʻAbd al-Nasir was in his inner self a man of peace despite his hard words. He was a man who wanted peace and bluffed war; whereas Israel wanted war and bluffed peace. Israel deceived the world by presenting itself as a weak, peace-loving nation threatened by the enmity of a state which surpassed her in numbers and blustered about a war to throw her into the sea. He who bluffs peace and wants war will win the war; he who bluffs war and wants peace will lose the war and lose the peace. That was our situation. . . .

We also listened during the famous Friday sermon to the reassuring news which the president announced about our success in the withdrawal of our armies from Sinai in the year 1956. They had been rushed there blindly at the beginning of the tripartite aggression. When the president saw disaster on the horizon, he immediately issued orders to withdraw. The retreat was completed in excellent order; he gave praise to God; and we praised Him too along with the president.

THE SAME STEP IN 1967

It appears that our president remembered this plan so well that he repeated it lock, stock and barrel in the 1967 war. In that war also, no sooner had disaster struck than he rushed to issue the now familiar order to withdraw! But how different were the two situations, circumstances and positions. During the tripartite aggression our army was in the early stages of its advance, and the attack was centred on Port Said; thus it was possible to withdraw the army successfully. In addition, the two greatest powers on earth were in agreement on the necessity of stopping the attack immediately and making the aggressors withdraw. This was the first time that, in the full view of an astonished world, those two had agreed on anything. Together they issued their well-known harsh warning, and the aggressors saw no way to avoid immediate retreat. The traces of the aggression were erased surprisingly quickly. The tripartite aggression quickly returned whence it had come so that everything returned to the *status quo ante* as though nothing had happened. But this tactic does not always work. In any case the phrase "erasure of the traces of the aggression" is not one to be committed to memory and thereafter easily realized. In the tripartite aggression the situation was different, for the two big lions did not want to let any of the smaller beasts dominate the Suez Canal and spread their influence in the Middle East. Together they blew a single puff and let out a loud roar which frightened the hyena, the jackal and the little fox. All fled leaving their prey behind in the ground. There was no power to them and no might. Port Said had fallen into the hands of the aggressors from their first leap, and its fate was sealed. Ismailia was within grasp of the claws and the incisors. But fear of the two lions made the claws and the incisors hesitate over the prey and turn their backs. . . .

THE PREY APPLAUDS "WE HAVE WON"

Then the prey, which had been saved by a miracle, woke up and began to shout to the high heavens, "We have won, we have won." It began to trumpet anthems which spoke in glowing terms of the Battle of Port Said, which was compared to the Battle of Stalingrad. In a way there was no damage or harm in that, for there is of course no shame in holding a lofty ideal up to the people. The damage comes when the aim is to deceive people rather than to raise their spirits and to play with the word *victory* in order to conceal from the people the causes of our inability to defend our soil. The bad results of that attempt appeared later. One of the results of deceiving ourselves and believing the lies which we broadcast about ourselves and the exaggerations which we made and gave free rein to in broadcasts, hymns and songs was that we began to get in the mood for military adventures.

THE ADVENTURE IN THE YEMEN

Hardly had the Suez Canal come firmly to rest in our hands in 1956 and had we begun to see our gold shining in our hand than we began to throw it at the hills of the Yemen,[65] for the Yemeni tribes which we wanted to attract to our side were only satisfied with gold. Gunny-sacks filled with the clinking yellow coins were rained on them from our airplanes. Tons of supplies and foodstuffs, whether slabs of fine cheese or cans of meat or fruit were also dropped from the air to our armies. But the burning sun and the absence of refrigerators spoiled these provisions, and they were abandoned in piles where they were dropped. Then the worms started to play in them, the smell of putrefaction hung over them, and no one would approach these piles. The hungry and deprived Egyptians did not know that this food of theirs, for which they had exhausted themselves, was the rendezvous of vermin in the dust of *Arabia felix*. Did we, all that considered, attract the tribes of Yemen with our gold? It is said that the tribes, even our clients, used to take our gold by day and fire on our officers and men by night. Then they hunted them, cut off their heads and sold them to the tribes of the other side. After that the Yemen affair ended. The whole débâcle was inconsistent with Egypt's political orientation. Some day the history of the Yemen war will be written in an honest way so that we will know the truth of what happened there. What was the result for which we had been ruined? What is now certain is that in addition to the lives that were lost from our armies (and according to what is said they are estimated in the tens of thousands of men), it is also known that the gold cover of the currency that we owned was totally lost in this losing war. With it was lost our hope of improving our condition.

A THIRD WAR AND A THIRD DEFEAT

Had we had enough with two wars and two defeats? No. . . . We had to have a third – the war and the defeat of 1967. That is, in a period of about ten years from 1956 to 1967 we exhausted ourselves, or more correctly, three wars and three defeats exhausted us. We do not know exactly how much they cost us, either in thousands of lives or in thousands of millions of Egyptian pounds. However, according to what has been mentioned and published, our losses in the recent wars alone are evaluated at about four billion pounds. As someone has said, had this amount been spent on the villages of Egypt, which number about four thousand, the share for each village would have been a million pounds. Such a sum would completely re-create the villages and raise them to the level of the villages of Europe. But our Egyptian villages have remained in their sad condition, and our poor peasants in their ignorance, disease and poverty. The billions, which came from the veins of Egypt to disappear into the morass, have disappeared. On top of that there was a reprehensible defeat. Indeed, on top of the reprehensible defeat more than five years have passed so far with Egypt suspended in a no-war no-peace situation and spending on her inactive army enough funds, as Muhammad Hasanayn Haykal has pointed out in an article in *Al-Ahram* of 21 July 1972, to build the High Dam twice or to build two High Dams each year which we could then tear down to fall into dust. . . .

WHAT JUDGMENT WILL HISTORY MAKE

What is this madness? What will history say about what happened during the era of this revolution? The revolution is the one that made certain charges about the regime of Khedive Isma'il[66] because he incurred debts of some thousands of millions which he spent in laying railroad lines, in building up the country, introducing new crops, and constructing palaces which have in any case remained for us up to now as installations used by the departments and ministries of government throughout the years. He also built other things such as the opera house from which we have benefited as a source for cultural and literary diffusion throughout the generations, and in still other things which at a certain time were called luxuriousness or stupidity, but which, to the degree that one can determine, were only manifestations of the contemporary civilization with which he wanted Egypt to catch up. . . . If history has pronounced *him* guilty, can we aspire to its absolving *us*? Personally, I hope that history will absolve 'Abd al-Nasir because I loved him from the heart, but I hope that history will not absolve a person like me, considered to be an intellectual, who, blinded by sympathetic attachment to the revolution, thus lost consciousness of what was going on around him. My confidence in 'Abd al-Nasir had made me interpret his conduct most optimistically and grope for some reasonable vindication of it. When from time to time certain doubts troubled my mind, and I feared that he had committed some excess or outrage, I would seek refuge in making him understand my view, from a distance and with compassion. I would write something from which he was to understand what I was driving at. One day I was afraid that the sword in the hand of the sultan would encroach on law and liberty, and I wrote "Al-Sultan al-Ha'ir".[67] Later, I was afraid that 'Abd al-Nasir was insufficiently aware of the feelings of fear and fragmentation that had struck Egyptian society before the war of 1967. I was afraid that he would rely on our society to go on another adventure, and thus I wrote "Bank al-Qalaq".[68]

All of these various writings, which were neither harsh nor bitter, constituted simply a warning, not an incitement. I learned that in fact 'Abd al-Nasir read them and understood what I intended. Obviously, however, he did not accept my views, but rather plunged forward on his own course. . . . Nevertheless, it was not easy to publish "Bank al-Qalaq". For more than half a year the work remained held up in the censorship which would not issue permission to publish it until those responsible heard that it might be published abroad, and they were absolutely forced to permit its publication. In addition, I did not shrink from writing about things as I saw them, even though they were considered dangerous. In the in-tray of one official are writings of mine which have not been permitted to appear up until now. Some of them were read secretly as *samizdat*. The pen cannot be silenced even with the existence of love and the absence of consciousness. We opposed and protested against corruption, in so far as we learned what it was, through writings which either have been published or the publication of which has not been permitted and also through direct transmission to those in power, verbally and in writing. But the problem did not lie here, for the individual voice is of little value no matter what its means and its courage. The problem is in the absence of a group voice representing the political, judicial, scientific, academic and cultural institutions. Where was their courage? Why did there not issue from them a voice or a movement, even symbolic, which would indicate to the absolute ruler that the country was conscious and pulsating with life? But they never moved themselves in defence of liberty or dignity either because they were indifferent or because of internal divisions amongst themselves. Nor am I free of guilt myself in this because I consider that my true guilt lies in my complete loss of consciousness of the situation even though I was of venerable age and had a mind which lived on thinking. The only interpretation of such lapses is that Egypt lived through a period which completely veiled the facts and hid the truth from her, at the same time that lies were promulgated by every medium of mass publication, broadcast and advertisement.

AN INDICATION OF THE MOCKERY

What happened to me on the fifth day of June 1967 and thereafter is one of the signs of that mockery which kindle surprise and astonishment. . . . I was ready to go out in the morning when all of a sudden the alarm sirens unexpectedly rang out. I figured it was only a test of the air-raid alarm system, and I went on out into the street. Everything was chaos. It was a real air-raid! The young volunteers of the civil defence were standing in the face of traffic and directing it from street to street, but traffic became tied up, cars were jammed together, and the entrances to the roads were blocked so that you did not know where to head. From time to time you would hear the rapid-fire shots of anti-aircraft guns.

I went to my office at *Al-Ahram* and found one of the office boys with a small transistor radio in his hand. Every quarter of an hour there was an announcement by those responsible in the war ministry or in the high command of the army to the effect that we had shot down one hundred enemy aircraft. By noon the number of downed planes had almost reached two hundred. By evening the number had climbed to I can't remember what number. I did not doubt but that the enemy's game was up. I walked the streets of Cairo from Liberation Square to Sulayman Pasha Square. Everywhere the Arab Socialist Union had put up big signs on which were written victory slogans such as "on to Tel Aviv. . . ."

The whole atmosphere around us almost convinced us that the entry of our armies into Tel Aviv would not be later than nine o'clock in the evening of the same day, 5 June 1967. But the next day arrived, and the military communiqués indicated the intensification of the battles in Sinai. I pictured the victorious movement of our armies in my mind. . . . When a visiting friend came by, he told me sadly, and much upset, that he had heard on foreign broadcasts that al-'Arish had fallen into enemy hands and that our armies were continually retreating. No alarm overcame me. I said calmly, with a smile, and with a tone of absolute confidence, "Listen . . . You don't understand the plan of our armies. . . . It is now clear to me that they do not intend to reach Tel Aviv or to penetrate deeply into the enemy's territory. They want only to lure their army deep into the Sinai desert and then to eliminate it. One reason is that the occupation of enemy territory would be a matter over which the United Nations and the Security Council would become excited, and the situation would end with a retreat from it as had happened to the enemy when he occupied Gaza and part of Sinai in 1956 and was then forced unwillingly to withdraw from them. Evidently, the destruction of his forces and the inflicting of heavy losses on him was a more important and more lasting goal in the view of our high command." This was the plan, and this was the secret of the retreat and the fallback of our ranks. I remained confident of this interpretation of mine. The next few days passed, and our forces were in a continuous retreat which resembled a rout. In the rush they abandoned all the positions from Sharm al-Shaykh to Rafah while I continued calm and smiling over my interpretation and the military plan which my imagination had constructed.

AN UNREASONABLE DEFEAT

My mind worked in that way because it was impossible, intellectually or logically, easily to believe that our armies could be routed in a few days. Years had passed during which the regime emphasised the army's marvels and showed us, whenever there was a revolutionary celebration, military reviews which included the latest models of tanks. During those parades we saw the rockets called al-Qahir[69] and al-Zafir[70] and saw units called al-Sa'iqah,[71] which ran snarling a frightening roar; we saw troops which dropped down from the heights, which hurdled over walls, and which literally tore up and ate snakes. . . .

We had also heard in speeches about the power of our aircraft which had no equal in the Middle East. We gazed up at swarms of them thundering in the sky, and for long years we had paid from the sweat of our brow national-defence and national-security taxes as surtaxes on top of the regular taxes which were carved out from the flesh of the Egyptian people, which deprived itself of much in order to support its army. The propaganda for this army made even those who were generally most dubious and pessimistic about the revolution say, as I heard personally from the mouths of such persons, "The revolution may be a failure in every way except, and truth demands that we admit the fact, for the army. This is true because the men of the revolution are fundamentally army men. It is the pillar of their existence, and they have spent on it what they have spent, and if everything in the society has turned bad at their hands, it is still not possible that the disorder should reach the army." Those who doubted the revolution said on the morning of 5 June 1967, "Yes, of course, our army will be victorious over the enemy. The army will win; that is a settled thing, but the proof is in the final result, and that could be a disaster if America were to intervene directly against Egypt." It was not, in short, possible for anyone, whether he was for the revolution or against it, to doubt the ability of the Egyptian army to check the enemy and conquer him. That certainty had increased even more the day we saw our president on television confronting those foreign journalists who had been assigned by the world's greatest papers to question him after the crisis had become grave following his closing of the Gulf of Akaba but before the outbreak of war on 5 June. What would he do if British or American warships came to open up the sea passage which he had closed? He responded with the confidence of a person who is in charge, "They will find there a force of which they do not conceive."

I did not doubt while watching that and hearing him on the television that there were atomic-tipped rockets in the offing. It never occurred to my mind that talk like that might be of the bravado type. Apparently, outside our country there were people who weighed the likes of that talk more accurately, for I heard, and I don't remember on what date, that a member of the American Congress had said while reading speeches of this kind by 'Abd al-Nasir, "This man is a bluffer." But not one of us in Egypt retreated a bit or even suspected the truth of what he set forth before us. Were we bewitched as I suggested above? Did it result from complete confidence in a leader on whom we had placed our hopes? Or was it that we had become used to the kind of life in which the revolution had placed us, a life in which we were stripped of any means of reception – inside a box which was locked on us by lies and delusions. . . ?

I kept on like that until Thursday, 8 June, living under the illusions of a great military plan. Every time the retreat of our armies was reported, my belief that the plan was being effectuated by decision increased as well as a belief that this retreat was an operational encirclement of the enemy's army – a wide pincer movement to tighten around it – until a friend called me on the telephone a little before midnight that Thursday to inform me that it had been officially announced in the Security Council or the General Assembly that Egypt had accepted a cease-fire. I woke up a bit: "How could Egypt accept that when she is winning?" Once again my mind exceeded all bounds, and I interpreted the affair to the effect that Egypt's acceptance of the discontinuance of the pursuit of its victories came about only at the request of America and on her promise to compensate Egypt with tempting aid in exchange for a cease-fire.

THE AMAZING TRUTH

I did not know the truth until Friday, 9 June, and as the truth dawned consternation seized me. . . . It appeared that we had lost the war in the first hours of 5 June. . . , and when we saw the face of the president on the television screen announcing the defeat and minimizing it by using the word *reversal*, we could not believe that we were in such a contemptible position and that Israel was in such a strong one. . . . It would have been more dignified on his part if he had not appeared in front of us on that day and had not spoken before us. Perhaps our minds would have enlarged the picture of his pain which it was impossible to bear. . . . But, nevertheless, we were moved, and he once more gained our sympathy by his knowledge of the fact and his statement to the effect that we are an emotional people. We forgot the defeat and began to dance, even in parliament, because of the simple existence of his person among us. What we should have done was to ask him, with kindness and love, the reasons for the defeat so that we might know our malady and thus prepare ourselves for health. This procedure would have been better than to have summoned him. In that case he would have concealed the disease and throttled the truth – and thus the corruption would have continued as it was – because of fear for the stability of his position. Of course the Egyptian people were not in a natural situation of consciousness like other people in similar circumstances who would question their leader at least with an ever-present consciousness. Nor do I say that he should have been tried or that the price of defeat should have been demanded from him as, for example, the French people did when they cursed Napoleon and left him in exile after the Battle of Waterloo while he began to renew his life by himself apart from the people. Despite the fact that the French leader was distinguished for glorious victories by which he mastered all of Europe, for the publication of the principles of the French revolution, and for the proclamation of European unity, they left him to pay the price for his one defeat, a defeat which was caused by one of his marshalls falling behind in following him in the battle. The marshall, Grouchy, lived unharmed while Napoleon bore all the guilt and the responsibility. . . .

In our case, despite the successive military defeats into which our eternal leader blindly plunged with the wealth of a poor people in order that at the end a small enemy should occupy his land, he remained to disavow his defeat, to make his marshall pay the price for him by committing suicide, and to dispatch his commanders to the courts and put the responsibility on them. Even those who wanted to write by allusion about corruption, defeat or decline had to keep the person of the president far from any responsibility; the responsible ones were always the others. Thus he continued in the seat of power in Egypt and in the Nasirist leadership over the Arabs generally – that leadership which ruined Egypt and brought tragedy to the Arabs. We had no means and no strength except to stick with him because he had stripped us throughout the years of every independent thought and of every strong personality other than his own. He succeeded in that to the degree that every personality in our country, even in the fields of science, thought and culture, began to feel his smallness next to a junior officer who was one of his aides. Thus he appointed to the presidency of the high council of universities and the high council for literature, arts and social sciences a young officer of quite limited education; our senior scholars began to sit politely before their chairman, the young officer, on their best behaviour. For with him rested the granting of honours and rewards: he could grant an honour to whomever he was satisfied with, or withhold it from whomever dissatisfied him. Some of those of whom our country should have been most proud, including Dr ‘Abd al-Hamid Badawi,[72] a legist of worldwide reputation who was deputy chief of the International Court at The Hague, were considered unsatisfactory. Badawi was disqualified for the state prize of merit despite his repeated candidacy put forward by those who knew his quality. The distinguished engineer, Dr

'Abd al-'Aziz Ahmad, had already been disallowed the prize for science on orders, despite the fact of his election by the flower of our learned men. In a similar way and despite his election, Dr al-Sanhuri, the author of the greatest encyclopaedia of law and the compiler of the laws of many Arab countries, was almost disallowed and would have been had it not been for the various efforts expended on his behalf, of which the most important were the efforts of Muhammad Hasanayn Haykal. Haykal prevented stubborn adherence to many evil deeds of that era, regardless of whether these shortcomings took place as a result of action by the leader himself or by his aides with or without his knowledge. This point is important because the responsibilities of important men are not diluted by motives or justifications. Because they are responsible for the fate of nations, they calculate the results only, and they bear them even when others have caused them. Furthermore, we always attribute the benefits and attainments to them just as we attribute to them evils and losses.

However, the leader was doubtless personally responsible for the appointment of the half-educated young officer as the director of the scholars and intellectuals of the country. This is also in contrast to Napoleon, for when he occupied Egypt accompanied by the cream of French scholars and established therein the Institut d'Egypte,[73] even he – the great Napoleon – did not have the audacity to appoint himself director of the Institut, but rather he made the famous scholar, Monge,[74] director and made himself merely Monge's deputy. There should be no surprise then that we should cling to our leader after the defeat and that we should make his personal existence a substitute for victory or synonymous with it. He had made us feel by every possible means that in Egypt and even in the whole Arab world there could only be found one single intelligence, one power, and one personality, namely 'Abd al-Nasir. Without him there would be nothing, no men, no intelligence, and no power that could be relied on; the only thing ahead would be ruin. Thus it was with Fascism, Hitlerism, and Nasirism; all of them stand on a single base which is the elimination of minds and wills other than the mind and the will of the leader. All of them, including Egypt, have seen the emigration of numerous minds abroad. And all of them leave a dominant shadow behind, and in their legacy are horses which greedy adventurers ride in their name. Verily, the idea of leadership of the Arab world is what has ruined us all and what possessed the thought of 'Abd al-Nasir and made of him a destructive force – destructive of himself, of Egypt, and of the Arabs. It is a lesson which we must grasp fully in order to combat anyone who may be tempted to leadership and domination of the Arabs by his person, his will, or his thoughts. In the end, our leader stayed as he had been submerging us under his habitual words about victory. The anthems repeating the word *victory* came back again, but victory had changed its meaning. It had come to mean the evacuation by Israel of the lands which it had occupied and their restoration to the *status quo ante* 5 June 1967. Yesterday, our national hope had been the end of the British occupation of our lands; today, our national hope is the end of the Israeli occupation of our land. Nevertheless, we continued reiterating the slogan of the revolution: "The way we were and the way we have become."

Days passed after the defeat. And every day the massiveness of its bulk became more clear to us – not by way of official announcements of the truth, but in convoluted ways, in fleeting and obscure lines slipped into a newspaper article. From such sources we understood that the army had been destroyed, including its weapons, equipment and its most modern tanks and planes, which had drained off Egypt's blood. They had been lost along with the lives, which were estimated at tens of thousands, and the treasure, which reached thousands of millions even though not a single shot had been fired. Senior officers of a friendly state said in amazement that had each tank stood fast and fired once, they would have inflicted losses on the enemy that would have made the war last for a reasonable period and would have made the defeat, if and when it happened, an honourable defeat. However, the well-known decision, the decision to withdraw, was at first glance – that is at first glance given the bad situation – the unique style which is our special stamp in the wars of the Nasirist revolution: getting ourselves entangled and then withdrawing.

But the withdrawal in the war of 1967 was at an exhorbitant price, horrible in appearance, in results, and in its vestiges. In fact, in the opinion of military experts it was a fearful human slaughter. The sudden withdrawal order given to a large army which was spread out in the desert and which had taken up its positions with its matériel over a period of weeks, and the appeal to this army to run barefooted without a careful, well-planned withdrawal and under the hail of enemy fire was a foolhardy decision from a responsible official who had lost his nerve. The official deserved to be tried, but that is not what happened. Egypt was pulverised in a rout so terrible that history will never forget it.

WHERE TO ERECT THE STATUE?

'Abd al-Nasir died three years after the defeat. We do not know how he was able to live through it. On the day of his death emotion overcame us all. Especially me. Feelings and considerations of loyalty moved me, and I suggested the erection of a statue to him in one of Cairo's squares. I received a number of approving letters from people moved like me by emotion and a few reluctant ones. Then I found among them one letter the author of which stated that he was in agreement about erecting the statue but that in his opinion its site should not be Cairo but Tel Aviv, because Israel should not dream that it could attain this degree of military power with such speed or that it could show the world such a superior level of civilization except by the grace of the policies of 'Abd al-Nasir.

THE REVOLUTION ENDS

It was natural for the revolution of 1952 to end on the day of the defeat, and in fact that is when it is considered to have ended in the view of history. What is intended here by the word *revolution* is of course the system which grew out of the revolution. It is usual for revolutions in the exact sense of the word to end at the moment of their transformation into a formal system of rule. For example, the revolution of 1919 ended after discharging its function and with the establishment of a type of royal parliamentary rule and the appointment of its leader as prime minister. The statement that the revolution of 1919 failed or ended with the undertaking of the revolution of 1952 is an inexact statement because the 1919 revolution ended thirty years before that with its transformation into a formal system of rule. Thus also the French revolution ended and completed its function with the conversion of France to the imperial system of rule in the period of Napoleon, and the Russian revolution fulfilled its task after Lenin took power and established his system of rule in a firm manner. Even the revolution that was Islam discharged its function with the establishment of Mu'awiyah[75] in power and its conversion, in the Umayyad period, into a dynastic system of rule. The situation was also thus in the revolution of Egypt in 1952. It fulfilled its function with the accession of its leader to the presidency of the republic and the establishment of the new system which made of the presidency of the republic an absolute presidency. This system, which was dictatorial in its essence and its true meaning, is what the defeat shook so strongly that the president described it as a fissure. It was natural that the fissure should get wider and that the system should collapse. What happened after that and up to now should be considered as a kind of emotional nervous contraction or a kind of motion sickness which accompanies the longing for the proclamation of the birth of a new Egypt.

AN OBJECTIVE STUDY

Whatever the case may be, this twenty-year period in Egypt's history will be the subject of exhaustive study. The period can, in fact, be divided into two stages. In the first stage rule was collective, and all those who participated in the revolution shared in it. This was the true revolution of 1952. The second phase was that in which 'Abd al-Nasir took over individual absolute rule after brushing aside the revolutionary council. It was this stage which may be dubbed the Nasirist revolution. I implore students of both phases that their guiding principles be justice and objectivity and that they not let any rancour, bitterness, conformism or emotionalism overcome their calm thought, their serious research and their composed judgment. They must bring out equally the good and the bad aspects of the revolution and its leaders. They must show them in their true dimensions. In addition, those who conduct such studies must not imitate the revolution of 1952 in the way that it belittled or ignored the revolution of 1919 and its men and overemphasized the importance of the 'Urabi revolution.[76] This attitude has suggested to some investigators the inferiority complex of the 1952 revolution and its prejudice against the revolution of 1919 simply because the latter was truly a popular revolution. Conversely, the acclaim and adulation of 'Urabi's movement may have resulted from its similarity to the revolution of 1952. The 'Urabi revolution was the movement of an army which rose up to demand certain specifics from Khedive Tawfiq[77] in much the same way that the revolution of 1952 was the movement of an army which demanded certain specifics from King Faruq. It was as though the irony of fate had willed that the comparison be complete, for the revolution of 1952 began to end with a military rout and a foreign occupation in just the same way that the 'Urabi revolution did.

Another thing that is unnecessary is for these studies to imitate the revolution of 1952 in its encouragement of falsification and hypocrisy and the obliteration of truth. Nor should they make the 1952 revolution out to be the birth date of civilization in Egypt and allow its claim that what came before it was the *jahiliyah*.[78] This point has special validity since the revolution of 1952 could not have taken place except on the strong pillars of a true Egyptian renaissance that arose in the thirty years prior to the outburst of the revolution. Hence it follows that our criticisms and attacks in what we have previously written about corrupt rule only applied to the men of power, whether king, politicians, or party chiefs, and not to Egyptian society as a whole.

WHO MADE THE STATE?

The corruption of power was on one side; Egypt with its intelligence, its strong arms and its free will was on the other side. The revolution of 1919 had this unusual characteristic: that it woke up Egypt, which then arose to search out its persona, to recover its spirit and its civilization by itself without relying on the rulers of Egypt, its governments, politicians and parties. After the revolution of 1919 Egypt itself, by its civilization, its thought, its art, and its economy, is what made Egypt. Its rulers did not make Egypt. But after the 1952 revolution Egypt was a product of the state more than of herself. The will of the state and the absolute decrees, issued without debate or opposition, were what directed everything in Egypt, even pure thought. This is the reverse of what happened after the 1919 revolution. When the political side of the 1919 revolution ended, the civilizational and intellectual revolution in Egypt began. The political revolution ended with the conversion of Egypt into a royal system of rule in which corruption began to appear year after year. But the intellectual and civilizational revolution began to move forward day after day, and its radiance and the solidity of its bases appeared without support from governments which were distracted from it by their party and political activities. The disinterest was true to the extent that I may illustrate it with the following point. The government did not even think about a literary competition which was announced in the twenties for playwrights. The one who thought about it and put up the money for its prizes was a private individual who paid out of his own pocket. In the 1952 revolution, politics, thought, civilization and every activity was undertaken by a single hand and emanated from a single head. That fact does not mean that everything that the revolutionary state did was wrong or that it was all devoid of benefit or goodwill. That is why I want the study of it to be based on the spirit of justice, equity and absolute objectivity. Egypt has known two systems over the last thirty years. One is a somewhat democratic system among whose faults (which we have noticed and criticized) are party wrangling and sterile quarrelling which obstruct beneficial projects and hold up their execution. Among its virtues are a certain freedom of speech, action, opinion and independent consciousness – minus foolhardy and dangerous gambles. The other system is built on absolute rule by the will of an individual. It has among its advantages rapid execution of what he sees as beneficial projects and among its faults precipitate decisions or a surprise built on foolhardy gambles which may embroil the nation in a single hour and introduce the source of its destruction.

EVALUATION OF THE ACHIEVEMENTS OF THE REVOLUTION

Thus if one day you submit to examination the achievements of the revolution of 1952, the examination must be of scientific objectivity and well removed from any emotionalism. For example, the agrarian reform should be studied in all its aspects. Did it stop at the point of limiting landholding and granting the landless peasant a certain number of feddans? Was it an agrarian reform in the true sense, as a result of which the mud huts which shelter the fellaheen disappeared and the picture of the Pharaonic peasant with his wooden plough vanished? Did modern equipment take its place and were draft animals freed from the backbreaking work as happened in true agricultural renaissances? Were livestock and flocks specially bred to supply the country with dairy products and meat? And what was accomplished in industrialization? What are its limits and its markets? What succeeded and what came to nothing – without puffery or bias? And socialism: what is the truth of its application and what are its limits? Is it just nationalization? Nationalization of riches, nationalization of liberties, nationalization of class struggle, nationalization of minds, and the putting of all that in one pocket, the pocket of the leader and in the circle of one politician, one economist, one intellectual – the person, the mind, and the will of the leader? Is his seizure of the properties and palaces of one class in order that they be occupied by another class with another name, but one which corresponds to the first in wealth and imitates its opulence – is that socialism? Are the people made happy because they hear socialist songs although they arc submerged in misery which everyone sees? This misery is seen not just inside their homes and their huts but also all over the streets where pressed masses of people wait for long hours in front of consumer co-operatives for a piece of meat to be thrown to them. These masses are aside from other deprived millions who could not recall the taste of meat; and aside from those masses of human flesh intertwined on staggering, broken-down buses in scenes which humanity rejects; and aside from groups of human beings who in filthy hospitals, receive the treatment of lost, neglected animals. Or take Arab unity – which emerged before the revolution in the feelings of those peoples in this Arab world of ours whose hearts were attuned to each other. It was proceeding on its course by natural means. Did the revolution succeed in bringing it about by political means? Did it bring it closer and strengthen it, or rather did it scatter and weaken it by policies which included intervention, pretension to leadership, domination, influence spreading, showering money in the planning of plots, fomenting *coups d'état*, and in the Yemen war inducing Arab to kill Arab, and Arab to use burning napalm and poison gas against Arab?! It is enough to note the opinion of Khruschev himself on the position of ʻAbd al-Nasir *vis-à-vis* the Arab states and Arab unity. He expressed his opinion in a letter to ʻAbd al-Nasir published in Muhammad Hasanayn Haykal's book, *ʻAbd al-Nasir wa-al-ʻAlam*. On pages 201–2 of that book, published by Dar al-Nahar in Beirut, occurs the following text:

> You will remember that in one of our discussions during your recent visit to Moscow you expressed dissatisfaction with the governments of the neighboring Arab regions, and you asked me what had to be done to change the internal situation in those regions which maintain a position of hostility toward the United Arab Republic and toward the aid which the Soviet Union can present to you in this respect [ʻAbd al-Nasir in another place in the letter had requested medium-range rockets from the Soviet Union], and as you remember, I answered you that the appearance of tolerance and forbearance from intervening in the affairs of other states is necessary. Influence in those regions will only result from a sound model and a good example on the part of the United Arab Republic, and that situation in turn will result from raising the economic and cultural levels of the people of your republic and their standard of living. Another factor would be the institution of a system toward that end which would enable all patriotic forces within the republic

> to exhibit its principles. I advised you to proceed to establish in the United Arab Republic those types of economic set-up and governmental system which by their nature would attract the other Arab regions so that their regimes would imitate the United Arab Republic in order to gain the affection of their own peoples. You smiled often that I was not realistic in examining the situation in the Arab regions. You added that affairs demanded more resolute management. I then answered you to the effect that intervention in the affairs of the Arab states was a very dangerous thing and that it was not in its nature that it lead to unity. On the contrary its nature would lead to the fragmentation of the efforts of the Arab regions. It appears, however, that I failed to satisfy you and that each of us maintained his own point of view in regard to this issue.

Thus it appears from the text of Khruschev's letter that even he himself saw in what 'Abd al-Nasir wanted to do something destructive of Arab unity. Or from a broad point of view take our culture, our schools, universities, instruction and our intellectual life in general. Did the levels in these areas rise or fall with the revolution? That is, did the Nasirist revolution improve the level of the economy of the people, of their culture, and of their comfort, as Khruschev had suggested? Did the revolution work for them as it had worked for leadership and domination over Egypt internally and over the Arabs externally? All these matters require just and truthful study.

Overall, did the revolution of 1952 bestow true benefit on Egypt and the Arab countries or was it a period obstructive of progress and renaissance? Was it a natural regime or an artificial regime which resulted from a movement which America had supported and planned in order to spread military regimes in this region on the model of what she had done in Latin America? The motive of the United States may well have been her expectation that Egypt at that time was really ready for and approaching a self-generating renaissance – a renaissance in which socialism was growing on a natural and popular basis and in which industrialization, reform and Arab unity stood on solid, sound foundations. Or was it perhaps the case that our country was still far from that and that there were no gains which could be obtained quickly except via military decisions?

All these subjects and questions must be an object of study by free thought and an objective mind. All the repeated and reiterated paragraphs on the attainments of the revolution are in need of a fine sieving far away from the drum and the horn, the anthems, songs and wordy slogans; and away from the inflation of the word *Nasirism* as though it were a theory!

THE LOSS OF THE CONSCIOUSNESS OF EGYPT

I assume that all these attainments are real, and with all my heart I hope that such a scrupulous study would confirm my assumption. But there is one loss about which there is no doubt and for which no attainment can compensate. I refer to the loss of the consciousness of Egypt. Imagine a man who controls his son and doesn't allow him any will or any choice over anything, who begins to shower him with all the bounties which he the father believes are proper for his son, who chooses for him the life-style that he should get used to and the wife that he must marry, and who supervises the newspapers that the son peruses, the books that he reads, the news that he hears, the songs that he sings, the films that he watches, the food that he eats, the medicine that he takes, the people that he befriends, and the enemies whom he forms. In short, imagine that the father makes sure that everything that relates to his son's intellectual, emotional and material life must run in the course which the loving father wants and prescribes without receiving from his son any consultation, opposition or free choice. What will the fate of the son be? Will the bounties and attainments which the father has showered on the son benefit him greatly when over the course of time he has been deprived of natural growth in his mental and volitional being and has become an individual of weak personality who has lost consciousness of himself, and is ignorant of the meaning of responsibility because he had never borne any by himself for a day? This result will come about because his loving father thought for him, chose for him, made all important decisions for him, and bore all responsibility for him, while he was sitting as though he were a retarded child who learned everything from the mouth of his father.

That was precisely my situation on the day that I sat in front of the television open mouthed like a moron listening to the collapse of revolutionary Egypt – a process which was complete in a few hours. But the drone continued in the accustomed way all around me: patriotic anthems, the songs of singers and songstresses, and company banners: victory, victory, victory, this Victory Company, that Victory Company, Victory Automobile, Victory Manufactury, Victory Store –

everything victory on victory on victory – to a laughable degree which could only provoke the derision of any reasonable person. But Egypt hardly reasoned and was unconscious of the fact that she had become a laughing-stock through these words and descriptions. She believed those who wanted to make her believe that she was living in a cornucopia of victories, victories of the revolution – all your days were victories. . . .

There was not a man among us who said or who could say: enough of your endless *victory* which is meaninglessly and unconsciously let loose over everything that happens to us. The country that has in fact had military, scientific or cultural victories does not overstate in this way and does not exaggerate by shamelessly reiterating this word in every single place with or without occasion. And anyway, defeats have come one after another; so what reason is there to continue doing something which provokes derision unless it is to keep on reassuring oneself that general consciousness has been lost. Could it be that the destruction of the consciousness of Egypt was a goal? After all, schoolbooks in the hands of the young so enormously inflate the glories of the revolution that one sniffs the aroma of falsification and flattery, and the very same books leave bright pages from the history of other eras in the shadow of the unconscious.

WHAT IS THE EXCUSE OF THE MATURE MEN?

But we, the mature men of the revolution, what is our excuse? What stupefied our minds? Some of us say that harsh measures were taken to prevent the formation of a public opinion free to debate and oppose and that there was stern censorship of everything that was published or broadcast. Then there were the imprisonments of those who were suspected of contrary opinions, accompanied by types of torture the reported horrors of which reached the level of legends. The truth of these charges no doubt must also one day be investigated. Regardless of the result, I must at least mention the torture of an outstanding university professor whom we knew, Dr ‘Abd al-Mun‘im al-Sharqawi.[79] He was subjected to bodily torture so ugly that his relatives and acquaintances denied its occurrence. He had been accused in a case of smuggling currency, and no sooner did he come out of the court with a verdict of innocence than he found an officer of the secret police waiting for him at the door in a car which led him to an unknown fate –

quite possibly to terrible torture. I no sooner learned of this affair from his brother, the poet, 'Abd al-Rahman al-Sharqawi[80] and from his professor, the late Dr Mustafa al-Qalali[81] – who had been unjustly punished by being removed from the university's governing council solely because he defended his student in court – than I immediately wrote a note in which I said, "This is a black stain on the face of the revolution which cannot be defended before history." I sent it to someone to deliver to 'Abd al-Nasir. Until then I had had a good opinion of him, and I did not believe that he was responsible. But rumours circulated that many people were being tortured amongst whom were some whose wives, daughters or sisters were brought in for the purpose of assaulting their modesty in front of them. We heard about all these atrocities, and our flesh crawled. Egypt had not known such things before. It was even said that these types of punishment were in the Hitlerite Nazi style and that in actual fact previous Nazi officers had been summoned to tutor the authorities in the various kinds of punishment. The strange thing is that this punishment could befall a university professor, but that the university would not bestir itself and that neither his colleagues on the faculty nor his students would protest if only by a minute's suspension of classes!?

It was the same on the day that there took place what came to be called the "massacre of the judges" because of the dismissal of some two hundred of them on trumped-up lying slander, unprotested by other judges. Another instance was the day that Dr al-Sanhuri, president of the council of state, was struck, humiliated, and almost killed without any protest by his colleagues.[82] A final example is that on the day the young officer was appointed our chief in the higher council of literature, we did not utter a word – not I, not Taha Husayn,[83] not al-'Aqqad.[84] Rather, we sat quietly as though the situation were natural. In this acquiescence, our responsibility – all of us, the cultured people – lay dormant, and the blame and indeed an accounting falls on us before history. All of us must be judged, and the file of the revolution must be opened in its entirety. Some will say that they were excesses based on repression and intimidation; others, that those who escaped from the intimidation and the repression fell into the snare of delusion. The reality is veiled, and a valid examination of these matters is blocked. There remains in front of us only a single perspective and a single picture, namely, what the powers of the revolution have drawn for us to the accompaniment of the beat of drums. They bewitched us with the glitter of hopes that had fascinated us for a long time, and they intoxicated us with the wine of "attainment" and "glory", and we got so drunk that we lost consciousness.

THE RETURN OF CONSCIOUSNESS

I have already mentioned the fact that 'Abd al-Nasir presented me with a copy of his *Philosophy of the Revolution* when it first appeared. In the dedication he alluded to my book, *'Awdat al-Ruh*, "calling for the return of another spirit in the age of the revolution". At that time it never passed through my mind that what Egypt would need twenty years after the revolution was not "the return of spirit" but "the return of consciousness".[85] It is a book that I myself will never write, not just because of my old age and poor health, but rather because my attitude toward the revolution had from the beginning been one of love, hope and forbearance, as I have mentioned in these pages, until the defeat of 1967 hit me in the face and revealed to me the seriousness of its defects. What then had I to do? What should my colleagues, the established writers do? Should we be silent, even when our consciences were asking why we were silent after we knew? Should we shout out? They would tell us that it was not the time for shouting, objecting and questioning. We would bandage our wounds and prepare ourselves for the coming battle "to erase the traces of aggression". Who then would write the book? Who could do that. . . ? As I see it, it has to be another writer from another generation, one who has the freedom and lack of emotional involvement which would enable him to make a clear examination and reach a firm judgment on an era in which the realities of things were confused to such an extent that certain key words and slogans were promoted and used in the opposite sense behind the curtain. For example, the words *freedom* and *the era of freedom* ran on tongues in speeches, songs and anthems at a time when no single free word which the ruler did not want could be expressed without its author entering prison. In fact the ruler succeeded in submerging all of Egypt within himself and in convincing Egypt, which had attained an age of more than five thousand years, that she was only as old as the revolution and its regime and that she had not existed before that. No doubt this point deserves mention. This skilful operation to compress mighty Egypt and seal it in the box of the revolution and its system suffocated Egypt and made it lose consciousness of the reality of its awesome weight throughout history and of all the previous systems which it had surmounted and yet remained Egypt.

Similarly, the hoped-for author will be better able than we to know with rigorous exactitude the truths that are totally locked away from us. He will be surprised when he learns that the burdensomeness of our losses of men and treasure in the Yemen war were only revealed to us in a few passing lines in a newspaper, and then only in 1970 or later. Or again, that permission for the passage of Israeli ships through the Gulf of Akaba remained hidden from us for a long time – from the year 1956 until President ‘Abd al-Nasir announced it in May of 1967. Or once more, that the person responsible for the losing wars and for the disaster embodied in the withdrawal order of the year 1967, which military experts consider to have resulted in an humiliating, destructive butchery of the Egyptian army, has not yet been made public. There are, in addition, many others of which we know nothing even now. All that we know is what we have seen with our eyes of the signs of the disintegration and destruction of our country and the misery of its people. When we began to feel the burdensomeness of the disasters of our revolution after the defeat of 1967, and when a kind of semi-consciousness began because of the necessity of a reckoning, there was immediately erected in front of us an impervious protective barrier encapsulated in the slogan, "No sound above the sound of the battle". Before the removal of the traces of aggression, no word would be proper. Otherwise, the speaker or the mover was acting against the fatherland. In that way the bonds were tightened again, and the mouths were sealed. Consciousness dissolved anew, and Egypt was not permitted to open the file on the case and judge for itself what had happened.

The significance of the return of consciousness to Egypt is the recovery of its freedom to judge things for itself. A fine example occurs to me of striving for the consciousness of the people. The day that de Gaulle came forward, he being a French national hero, for the referendum on the presidency of the republic, five candidates came forward with him. Before the public referendum all of them were permitted an equal opportunity to put forward their programmes in the press and the media. One of the papers published five columns headed by numbers but not names. In each the programme of one of the candidates was placed, and the paper invited its readers to choose the programme without knowing its author. The names of the candidates were only mentioned on the last page. I wanted to try this operation out for myself. I chose one of the columns. The programme in it astonished me. I turned the paper over to learn the name of the one I had chosen. To my utter surprise it was de Gaulle himself. . . .

This is the way a free public opinion is trained. They strive for the consciousness of the people in that country. The meaning of referendum when all the papers thump the drum for the word "yes" in heavy red type and where the result comes out as a 99.9 per cent vote in favour, is that the country has no consciousness, no freedom, and finally no human dignity.

Will Egypt one day recover a free consciousness? To that end the book *'Awdat al-Wa'i*[86] must some day be written. . . . But it will never be written until the file of truth is opened. . . .

All the truth, from 23 July 1952 until the present time – 23 July 1972. . . .

A Word in Memory of 'Abd al-Nasir

(*Al-Ahram*, 28 September 1974)

My opinion about the cure for all this is that it is dependent on a general change taking place in Egypt's social milieu in all its aspects, political, ethical and religious. Now, neither the school nor the home can do very much to reform what has been corrupted because the corruption has come from a devastating[87] storm based on distorted principles badly understood which burst suddenly on the country and, as we have seen, turned it upside down in the worst way. Furthermore, the matter is greater and more dangerous than is curable by patch-work cures. What is required is nothing less than another overpowering storm based on sound and true principles, a storm which must arise, put up what has fallen, and repair what has been ruined. The difficulty, however, is how and when the blessed storm will come. In my opinion it will not come without advance preparation unlike the way that first destructive storm came. That storm entered stealthily through a window opened by a long and glorious struggle and a glorious national movement. The role of the home and the school lies in this advance preparation. On them falls the burden of making the young people understand that the situation in which they are cannot last and that they themselves must prepare for whatever reforms are needed. Home and school are responsible for increasingly calling the attention of the youth to lofty high examples and sound ethical principles. Home and school must also point out to the youth its own shortcomings, the shortcomings of the generation, and the sickness of the age. These institutions must satisfy them that they are the ones on whom the country will depend to reform all this corruption one day and to bring about the blessed revolution which will establish the fatherland on a basis of health, strength, and system. . . .[88]

(The above is a page from my book *Shajarat al-Hukm* published in 1945.)

Seven years after these words were written, the "blessed revolution" took place, the revolution of July 1952. It was natural for me to receive it both with surprise and with warmth. After all, my prophecy had come true. It was as though I had written down the future of the fatherland and then there had taken place a partial implementation of what we had sought by way of social justice, limiting land ownership, and machinery on the road to socialism. Then 'Abd al-Nasir appeared, and his personality crystallized into the repository of hope. Between him and me the bonds of heart-felt love were consolidated, although from a distance because throughout his life we did not meet for more than a few minutes while standing. It did not happen that we ever sat down together or that we had a long session together. However, as I learned, he used to value me and to consider me almost a spiritual father of the revolution which I had prophesied and advocated. This personal side I shall continue always to treasure in my heart, and I shall bear it in the depths of my soul as a most beautiful memory.

The personal side is my right; but the public side is the right of the fatherland. When I wrote in the forties about the necessity of the outbreak of a "blessed revolution" the impulse was to reform the condition of the fatherland. In fact we gave the revolution our support, and we gave 'Abd al-Nasir our love and our warmth to such a degree that he should have felt secure enough to raise our country to the highest level of civilization and welfare. My hope had been that I might see illiteracy disappear in our country and an end to the mud huts in which the Egyptian peasant lived without toilets, urinating and excreting like an animal in the wild. My hope had been that this peasant might begin to live like a human being, that the Egyptian worker might have available clean hospitals for his use and worthwhile sports clubs for his and his family's free time; in short . . . that he be raised to a social level similar to that of the likes of him in the developed countries. My hope had been that the whole people should benefit from what we had prophesied for it at the hand of a "blessed revolution" which would stand on the feet of health, strength and order. To what degree and to what extent did the people enjoy these attainments? In my opinion the attainments on behalf of the people which were realized by the actual revolution did not exceed ten per cent of what we had expected. I shall be optimistic and increase my estimate to twenty or thirty per cent, but in terms of our freedom, our consciousness, our lives and our monies, the expenses were at the most exhorbitant prices. Whatever the figures, our hopes for the revolution had been greater than what has been realized up till now.

'Abd al-Nasir ruled the country absolutely and individually for approximately fifteen years during which he should have been able to stabilize the country on sound, secure socialist and democratic bases. If he had succeeded, we could now be harvesting its true fruits not its external trappings. What happened? No doubt he wanted the best for his people, but what prevented the realization of this "best" was a combination of obstacles, deficiencies, means and impediments. What exactly were they? We must know all of that so that we can find the cure and resume the march toward guidance and light. For the sake of this we demand and we shall continue to demand the opening of the file.

I do not know why there is anger, fear, horror and alarm on the part of some people at the mere mention of the file and examining the file! Is it personal fear of a secret they do not want uncovered! Or is it a sort of worship of an individual whom we have become used to and the touching of whom we consider as apostasy? Or is it because of a decline in national education "which does not distinguish between debate and attack"!? From the whole experience of people does it follow that difference of opinion leads to concentration camps!?

"Difference of opinion does not corrupt friendship" is a proposition the wisdom of which is ancient. How nice it would be if the people understood it and acted by it. In the field of politics it is the summit of ripeness; in the area of personal relations it is the cause of the soul's rest and of freedom of view. I do not know what is wrong with it if I love the person of 'Abd al-Nasir as a friend while I examine his public actions as a citizen? Why do we always confuse friendship and opinion, personal feelings and public positions and consider every criticism a private feud? One day when I wrote a rebuttal to an opinion which was said to be that of Ustadh[89] Haykal, those who knew of the friendship between us were surprised and thought that it was a personal feud. They did not know that we always disagree when some meeting brings us together and that I had previously roughed him up twice as harshly as I did in what they read. Beyond that, neither of us hesitate to seize the other by the forearm and at the same time we continued taking our meals together in a pure spirit and with real friendship.

There is, in fact, an argument worthy of notice which is the claim that any criticism of the revolution of 1952 or any intrusion on Nasirism is an apostasy which threatens the attainments of the people and takes us backwards. If that were true, it would in fact be a tragedy. Furthermore, if the proposition means that we should sit back chanting the praises of the revolution and of Nasirism, singing of gains with which we are content and with whose perfection we content our souls, blinding ourselves to the revolution's failures, and not demanding more from it (plus reform of that which was corrupt in it), well, that would be another tragedy. . . .

Therefore, it is the responsibility of the people and especially of the youth that they choose between contentment and worship on the one hand and aspiration and liberty on the other, between that worship of the individual which blinds one to thought, and reflective and free aspiration toward a future of wide horizons. . . .

I specify the youth because I have directed my words to them and because for thirty years I have pinned on them my hopes for bringing about "the blessed revolution". My hopes for the youth of that period were not disappointed, for that revolution did arise through their efforts. I am today an old man nominated for death at any moment. I have no ambition and no hope for anything. For me the most suitable thing is to sit comfortably, calmly awaiting the end. What then impels me to do what I am now doing? No doubt the situation in which I find myself is particular to me, namely, that I am the prophet and the advocate of "the blessed revolution". I must answer this question: has this "blessed revolution" realized all the hopes and dreams which many expected that it would realize for the fatherland? It was to answer this question that I wrote *'Awdat al-Wa'i* on the twentieth anniversary of the undertaking of this revolution. . . .

All of this is the claim of the fatherland on me. As for the claim of personal love and friendship, it necessitates that I mention with charity a man who kept my friendship all his life and on the day of whose death I could not restrain myself from shedding honest tears. As long as a day of remembrance is held for his passing, I shall appeal for mercy and forgiveness for him from the depths of my heart.

[*signed*] Tawfiq al-Hakim

Samples of the Reaction to *The Return of Consciousness*

True Courage

(Muhammad Hasanayn Haykal, *Majallat al-Sayyad*, Beirut)

Everybody who has written and everybody who has spoken was present during the days of ʻAbd al-Nasir and could testify about them. The easiest possible thing to say to them is that they were spectres – weak and frightened spectres. He who is courageous does not wait for death in order to put his courage into operation. True courage is that a man stand before life and compete. He who can only whisper his opinion after death and until he has made certain that no one will reply does not have a position in which there is any kind of courage. In addition, I am very sorry to say that there was no one who was quicker to burn incense before ʻAbd al-Nasir than those who have written memoirs. By extension the same remark applies to their overall positions. The strange thing is that the defenders of Nasirism these days are the people who had during ʻAbd al-Nasir's lifetime critical opinions about some aspects of the experiment. But those who now speak up against the experiment and make heroes of themselves are shamed both because they were silent during ʻAbd al-Nasir's life and because they attack him after his death.

I do not believe that anything can affect ʻAbd al-Nasir. ʻAbd al-Nasir will remain the natural offspring and the true expression of the Arab nationalist movement in the twentieth century, and Nasirism will continue to be the programme for the development of the Arab nation – a programme which is capable of development and which is not frozen. I cannot see a future for the Arab world or for the developing world as a whole without Nasirism, the collection of ideas, the implementations, and the Nasirist efforts which are the basis for anything undertaken. Probably something will be published about "Egypt and the Defeat", that is, that ʻAbd al-Nasir was defeated in 1967, but this is not a serious problem. ʻAbd al-Nasir will remain an expression of Egypt and of the Arabs at a particular stage to the same extent that Napoleon is a particular expression of France. There is, of course, a difference. Napoleon's part of the movement was only an offshoot of the revolution, even if there were attempts to portray his portion as though it were the revolution itself. But ʻAbd al-Nasir's orientation from the first day to the last was toward change, the future and history.

He was defeated? We agree. But the strange thing is that some people consider, for example, that Suez[90] was his defeat. That's how far the distortion of history reaches.

Suez was a fundamental movement for all of the third world: Africa, Asia and the Middle East were all different after Suez. If the Arabs are talking about their wealth these days, Jamal 'Abd al-Nasir was the first who stood in the face of the monopolies and, by nationalizing the Suez Canal, became the first who gave dignity to all the Arabs.

During the lifetime of 'Abd al-Nasir, his strength and the strength of his *élan* and his dignity inhibited a true dialogue with his thoughts. On this day I feel warmly towards this apostasy against 'Abd al-Nasir because it will generate real contact with his thoughts.

'Abd al-Nasir was an hypothesis presented for consideration, an hypothesis which imposed itself with strength and swept away very many things.

I believe that we shall in the end arrive at a confirmation of the fact that everything that 'Abd al-Nasir advocated in regard to principles and ideas is sound.

There were errors in execution, but where in all the world do errors in execution not take place?

People stop at the errors in execution and forget the accomplishments. This is unreasonable.

Tawfiq al-Hakim's Rejoinder

(*Akhbar al-Yawm*, Cairo)

It attracted my attention that Ustadh Haykal, the defender of 'Abd al-Nasir, responded to himself by himself when he described those who today criticize the rule of 'Abd al-Nasir as weak, frightened spectres. It is true, but does one find weak, frightened spectres anywhere except in an atmosphere of terror and fear?

Why are weak, frightened spectres not found in countries like France, England, America, Sweden, and other countries whose people do not live in fear and anxiety about torture, concentration camps, killing, the distension of bellies, and aggression on the honour of wives, daughters and sisters, along with deforming opposing views by sullying them with accusations of plotting and treachery?

In regard to the courage of today's critic who criticizes because he is certain that no one will ever rebut him, such conduct in truth would not be courage, but the reality is different. The fact is that the response, the harsh response full of personal defamation, falls today in most Arab countries only on those who dare to question the sanctity of ‘Abd al-Nasir.

Indeed, many newspapers in the Arab world treated my book *‘Awdat al-Wa‘i* as an ugly defamation of my person. Therefore, let Ustadh Haykal put his mind at ease because he who questions the sanctity of ‘Abd al-Nasir, whether in Egypt or elsewhere, will find those who will rise up to defend him with both truth and falsehood.

The fact is that everywhere those who ride on the charger, ‘Abd al-Nasir, are always the greatest gainers.

Therefore, let the question of courage be put aside, for the question is not a question of courage, especially for some people, but the question is one of judgment, and for me anyway it is also a question of love and friendship. I love the person of ‘Abd al-Nasir and I feel friendly toward him for many reasons of which many are aware. Perhaps the most important is that he used to love me and respect my opinions down to the last moment of his life. From the beginning of his regime he brought together my opinions and his opinions, my hopes and his hopes. He always supported me, and it was natural that I should always defend him.

Indeed, I did.

To the extent that the whispering of frightful accusations grew up around me. They began to increase daily and at times to reach the extent of crimes for the commission of which the laws and regulations punish perpetrators to the limits of severity. What, therefore, is the position that every friend who sees frightful accusations measured out against his friend should and would take? Should he be satisfied with denial, cover-up, pretence and the defamation of everyone who criticizes the friend? Or should he rather seek an honest fair investigation so that his friend can emerge with an acquittal?

I chose the second course – in order to fulfil my nature and my first profession as a man of the law. Thus I wrote the pages of *‘Awdat al-Wa‘i* for myself. I outlined my personal opinion on the subject without intending to publish them at that time, but subsequently they got out of my hands and were published.

These pages do not constitute a bill of indictment or some kind of judgment because that would necessitate the existence of documents and the revelation of truths. They are merely a request for a minute investigation of accusations made against a person that I like and felt friendship for, but since this person was also a symbol of the nation, a public assessment of him becomes a right of the nation.

No nation in the world is conscious if it permits a heavy curtain long to conceal from it the truths which bear on the person who shaped its fate and continued to shape it even after his death. The portrayal of 'Abd al-Nasir today as a weak, lifeless, forgotten corpse on which the claws of those who would demonstrate courage have pounced is a false portrayal. On the contrary, he is an unshakeable force to whom imposing statues have been erected in some Arab countries and in whose name prizes are awarded in others; he is a lofty portrait on the walls in Egypt and everywhere.

Therefore, the portrayal of him as having died and passed into oblivion is the portrayal of an interested party who wants to keep the claws from exhuming the truth, a step which might uncover something that the self-interested would prefer to keep hidden. In a similar way, the attempt by his defenders to defame personally anyone who wants an investigation is an aberration which arouses suspicion. Not once has a defender got at the essence of the issue. The twisting and turning which surround it are all according to the well-known courtroom technique in which slanderous questions rain down: "Where were you then?" "Why didn't you say that before?" "What made you be silent until just now?" *et cetera . . . et cetera*.

Old, familiar tricks to obfuscate the accusation, to divert attention from the essence of the charge, and to get the accused off. Despite these tricks the essence of the accusations and the truth of the crimes always continue to stand, and the question remains:

Did they happen or not?

Were they committed or not?

Here is the essence of the question. Here is the whole issue. Let him who possesses a serious answer come forward with documentation. Anything else is vituperation and sloganeering. What I aim for is the facts so that my heart may be at ease over someone who was dear to my soul. If his innocence is confirmed, I shall be the happiest of people. If he be convicted, I shall bear the responsibility with him, and I shall thereby be proud because I shall have rendered the judgment which has returned to the nation its consciousness.

Those who really love 'Abd al-Nasir will demand the opening of his file so that their hearts may be at ease as a result of his clean record. Most of those who ride the 'Abd al-Nasir charger do not want any approach to the steed, and they disfigure with their lances the person of anyone who touches him because the only thing that concerns them is riding the charger.

Many of Nixon's friends and members of his party wanted him to be tried. They did not ward off any accusations which might arouse suspicion or doubt about his name because they knew that the silencing of doubt by certainty was in his interest and in the interest of national consciousness. Whatever 'Abd al-Nasir's value and the value of his services, he was a created being and a citizen who does not have to have an untouchable beatification or an eternal immunity which defies the revelation of the truth.

This is the significant thing, which must finally be established in the minds of all who love 'Abd al-Nasir in a true and not in a self-serving way, of all who esteem him, and of all who appraise him at his true value.

A Journalistic Question

(*Al-Musawwar* magazine, Cairo)

Some of the pens which have been raised to attack you have not opposed the steel of what appeared in the book . . . and indeed you yourself confronted the question which is posed: why didn't you answer it at the time with a reputable reply . . . ? You said that conditions did not permit anyone to find a platform from which to publish his point of view and, likewise, that we were not given knowledge of the implications of the enormity of some of what happened.

This is reasonable . . . , but . . . didn't phenomena appear which we should have confronted?

The Response of Tawfiq al-Hakim

Those pens that take refuge in the satisfaction of attacking me without opposing the steel of events are following the mistaken belief that defaming the person may cover and hide the truth of the events. But there is no escape from uncovering, some day, the facts. My person is transient but what concerns the nation is permanent. To answer the question, "why the silence up to now?" let me say that everyone who asks that question knows perfectly well the reason for the silence. If we assume that silence about a crime is sinful, what should be said about the perpetrator of the crime? Should we forget the perpetrator of the crimes and settle accounts with the one who was silent about them? At least, try both of them. Settling accounts with the critic who was silent and covering up the criminal who committed the crime has another meaning, another designation, and another cause. Your question, "didn't phenomena appear which we should have confronted?" is quite proper. Indeed, there were phenomena which compelled me to confront them with the means which I had available. Among them was the phenomenon of the throttling of freedom and the phenomenon of giving the law a vacation. In this matter, I saw it as my duty to write "Al-Sultan al-Ha'ir" so that I could clarify the obligation to respect the law and freedom and to avoid using the sword and violence. In it there appears this sentence as a warning to the ruler: "The sword imposes your rule, but it exposes you; whereas, although the law constrains you, it protects you." Verily, that which really protects the ruler is law and liberty. The danger, to which he cannot stand up, is the sword which he thinks will protect him. I wrote "Al-Sultan al-Ha'ir" in 1960 when this phenomenon began to become visible. Another phenomenon appeared in 1966. It was the phenomenon of apprehension in Egyptian society, which spread to such a degree that our society apparently lived without a spinal column. It was a society which had sagged, rotten and jellylike and hence was not suitable to confront any external force. I feared at that time the result of some uncalculated military adventure relying on a sick, sagging, apprehensive home front. As a warning I wrote *Bank al-Qalaq*, but despite all that no attention was paid to these books, warnings and confrontations; then the forbidden happened.

A Letter from Tawfiq al-Hakim to the Egyptian Left

(*Ruz al-Yusuf*, Cairo)

After the first shock created by *'Awdat al-Wa'i* had passed, along with the superficial and formalistic reactions that the book had stimulated, especially in certain Arab countries in which commercialized Nasirism reigned, I thought that now the time had come to enter into the core of thc issue which had caused it, and to debate the essence of the subject at a certain distance from persons and personalities.

I seek in my discourse here to address the left directly because I – whatever my ideals are – consider myself one of the people responsible for Egyptian socialism.

I know very well the present position of the left and of the Nasirist left in particular. I know its fear of exploitation by reactionary forces in criticizing the accomplishments of 'Abd al-Nasir. But this fear of the left can almost land it in a reactionary position! For it forgets the crisis of democracy which took place [in Egypt] in the years 1953–4, and it forgets its own position in rejecting the totalitarian regime which was in power in those years. It is true that the position and orientation of the revolution differed after the nationalization decisions, but the left should let up a little on its embellishment and gilding of our experiment in socialism and its portrayal of it as the ideal socialism!

Perhaps the excuse of the left for this position is its fear of a backward apostasy to something worse. In that case, it is a tactical position required by the necessities of the present circumstances and not a sound, solid strategic position to be continuously maintained because the claim that Nasirism is true socialism is a falsification of reality and of history. As is the case with every falsification there can be no escape from the fact that it will collapse and be uncovered. This eventuality will certainly lead to the appearance of a left true to itself and to truth. This left will build its ideology and its struggle on true socialist ideology without borrowing old clothes. In order to protect the future of the left in Egypt, attention must be given to this goal from now on before the falseness of the present temporary, tactical position becomes clear to the eyes of sincere socialists.

In what I have written I have not charged 'Abd al-Nasir with a crime as people say. On the contrary I love him and I esteem him. But I do put his efforts in their place, and I consider that the difficulties of democracy and socialism in our country continue – after 'Abd al-Nasir – to need other solutions, revolutionary and democratic.

I do not criticize at the expense of the past but only for the account of the future.

I have attempted to criticize what I cannot accept of the negative sides of the days of 'Abd al-Nasir – which includes the days of al-Sadat as well.

My progressive tendencies have always been clear, including the period before the revolution. It is enough to mention my anti-Nazi book *Sultan al-Zalam*[91] which was written forty years ago.

My attachment to Marxism, which I studied in the twenties when the Russian revolution was less than seven years old, is well known. In those days we observed the formation of a clear socialist party or tendency in Egypt.

For all these reasons, I consider it my right to speak today about socialism in Egypt and my right to act to place it on a sound basis and to be concerned for the Egyptian left and to guard it and its future.

I blame this left because it is now completely incompatible with itself and because it is in a state of apostasy from the true essence of socialism. I say this because of its concern with temporary tactics at the expense of the true socialist programme and at the expense of the independence of a platform which is distinguished by the formation of an alliance which serves opportunism more than it serves the workers, the intelligentsia and the peasants.

The left's fear of the return of old-fashioned reaction makes it fall – as I said – into the service of new-style reaction.

I believe that the left must criticize the many negative things that we have endured. It is its duty.

The incompatibility of the left with itself will redouble when we see the present leadership announcing that it is a partner responsible to the past leadership. What then is to be defended? Against what? What should be disavowed and what embraced?

The story of *'Awdat al-Wa'i* is simply that in 1972 on the occasion of the celebration of the twentieth anniversary of the July revolution, I found myself in a difficult crisis at the moment of withdrawal from my intellectual life which is also the life of modern Egypt – Egypt, around which all my writings, studies, and indeed the voyage of my life had revolved.

What had the revolution done to us? What had it done for us?

To answer this question I wrote my impressions in *'Awdat al-Wa'i*.

What matters to me now is that I confirm and that the Egyptian left understand that the essence of *'Awdat al-Wa'i* is the examination of an era, or more accurately an appeal for the examination of an era, after it has become a part of history – a history whose details, truths, secrets and records continue to be unknown. It is a mistake in such a situation to delay bringing authoritarian regimes out into the open – whether they be regimes of the right or of the left! There is, therefore, no way to avoid opening the whole file of the revolution of 1952.

15 October 1974

After Tawfiq al-Hakim's Letter to the Egyptian Left: a Letter of Rebuttal

Not One Marxist Attacked You!

('Abd al-Sattar al-Tawilah, *Ruz al-Yusuf*, Cairo)

After Khruschev delivered the speech in which he disclosed – before the Communist Party congress of 1956 – the abuses of liberty under Stalin, members of the congress began to present written and signed questions to him. One was a question which said, "If this abuse of democracy took place at the time of Stalin, where were you?"

Khruschev read the question and noticed that it was unsigned. He called, "Who is the author of this question?"

But no one answered.

Khruschev then laughed and said, "My answer is that I was like you, the author of the question!"

Then he added: "Don't forget that the torture under Stalin led in a single year to the death of two-thirds of the members of the central committee on the charge of treason!"

This story turns around in my mind whenever I hear an attack on one of our greatest writers, Tawfiq al-Hakim, the author of *'Awdat al-Wa'i.* For the most part this attack has centred on two formalistic questions.

First: How did consciousness return to the author after twenty years and after the immortal leader 'Abd al-Nasir had died, and why was he silent throughout this period about the mistakes with which his book dealt?

Second: Some of what he wrote is contradictory to what he wrote during the life of 'Abd al-Nasir.

Although I do not know Ustadh al-Hakim other than through his writings and do not agree with most of what he has written in *'Awdat al-Wa'i*, nevertheless I see the attack which is now being mounted against him as unfair and wrong.

If we assume that al-Hakim has been afraid for twenty years, it is his right to be afraid. He does not claim to be the leader of a party or a member of a party or the bearer of a gun. It has happened in all countries of the world, not just in Egypt, that thousands of people have been frightened in certain circumstances. Then, when the opportunity presented itself, they talked. The rightness or wrongness of al-Hakim's views will not be decided by whether or not he was afraid.

It is certain that many of those who are attacking him today themselves knew fear as he did. It is known and understood that most of the Egyptian intelligentsia were whipped on the back throughout the last twenty years, either directly or indirectly; it is clear that the whip frightens.

We cannot forget here the caravan of two thousand Egyptian citizens who were chained on their way into exile in the desert camps and in the Abu Za'bal prison[92] one night in 1959 because they were the only ones who said no!

The contradiction between what Tawfiq al-Hakim writes today and what he used to write yesterday is also a weak argument because as long as there is no definite indication of hypocrisy, it is plausible that the man has, based on the fact of his experience, changed his mind. The Egyptian left – and Marxists in particular – have, some of them, twice erred in appraising the revolution of 23 July, and have then changed their minds.

Therefore, the opinions of Tawfiq al-Hakim must themselves be debated with objectivity, kindness and friendship.

Above and beyond the impressive literary position – Arab and worldwide – which Tawfiq al-Hakim enjoys, we must be pleased at his entry in a direct way and at an advanced age into the field of politics. In addition to his riding the difficult mount, according to his declaring – and for the first time – his attachment to Marxism (*Ruz al-Yusuf*, 21 October), this act represents high courage on his part at a time when numerous voices are raised which freely contribute to a harsh attack (brutish and scorching, in fact) against Marxism without any special occasion.

Verily, we are in the presence of a writer who has warned us against Fascism for forty years and who has recorded his commitment to the love of Egypt in his writings. Therefore, it is incumbent on patriots, and especially on the leftists among them, to use a fraternal approach when criticizing him.

In fact, al-Hakim struck the heart of the truth in his letter directed to the Egyptian left when he said that the left's fear of reactionary exploitation of criticism of the accomplishments of 'Abd al-Nasir might lead to our landing in a reactionary position.

Anyway, it is not possible for a leftist to defend concentration camps, torture, prisons and violations of democracy. His responsibility is to criticize all of this, but his difficulty is to limit the extent to which he should plunge headlong into criticism and to find a framework suitable for it.

The right criticizes the accomplishments of 'Abd al-Nasir and the regime of Anwar al-Sadat as well, but we know very well that the clear enemy of democracy is the right. What it wants is a democracy of the new elite, plus an onslaught on the accomplishments of ‘Abd al-Nasir, on the regime of al-Sadat, and on the whole revolution of 23 July.

The Egyptian right views the regime of al-Sadat as a transitional stage during which it will be able to exploit the present democratic liberties to put an end to the revolution once and for all.

But does the rightist attitude mean that the left should refuse democracy?

In fact, the left itself – especially Marxists – used to criticize the negative aspects of the Nasirist experiment in no uncertain terms and indeed suffered more than any other nationalist group the results of this criticism: years in prison, torture, dispersal and . . . *etc*.

This left was confronting torture and repression while asserting the nationalism of the regime and extending its hand to it in co-operation – despite the fact that this hand met only the whip and a heavy truncheon. But the left continued to hold out its hand while its tongue was criticizing the negative aspects of Nasirism.

This sound position has been the position of the Marxist left up until now, even regarding the negative aspects of the present stage.

Therefore, when al-Hakim says that the left embellishes and beautifies the Egyptian socialist experiment, he is incorrect.

It is, in fact, incorrect to say that the Marxists – and they *are* one division of the left – describe the experiment of ‘Abd al-Nasir as though it were ideal socialism. No Marxist would make this statement.

Indeed, what the Marxist left has always said is that the Arab Socialist Union in its present status serves opportunism more than it serves the workers and peasants, and that the problems of democracy and socialism in our country will continue to need after ‘Abd al-Nasir's time (as they did during his regime) other solutions both revolutionary and democratic.

Perhaps al-Hakim will forgive some of the leftists who have participated in the attack on him because their participation was a reaction to the frenzied attack of the right which had a very loud voice and numerous platforms.

It is true that at times their reaction took on a nervous, convulsive form which harmed the essence of the Nasirist experiment more than it benefited it.

But . . . I must register the fact that so far I have not read a single attack by a leftist Marxist writer on Tawfiq al-Hakim.

Tawfiq al-Hakim can write whatever he wants . . . and all nationalist forces should receive what he writes magnanimously . . . and debate him calmly. . . .

How much the nationalist forces have exerted themselves in various struggles against one another while the right and imperialism watched, applauded and prepared an onslaught against all in order to deliver a *coup de grace* after they had exhausted themselves . . . and some had weakened others by inflicting wounds.

Notes

NOTES TO TRANSLATOR'S INTRODUCTION

1. It should be noted that Islamic fundamentalists in Egypt had rejected 'Abd al-Nasir's nationalist ideology from the beginning and had been driven underground.
2. The major collection of articles and debates opposing *'Awdat al-Wa'i* is in Tawfiq al-Hakim, Lutfi al-Khawli *et al.*, *Malaff 'Abd al-Nasir: Hiwar al-Yasar al-Misri ma' Tawfiq al-Hakim* (Beirut: Dar al-Qadaya, 1975). See also the important work by Luwis 'Awad, *Aqni'at al-Nasiriyah al-Sab'ah* (the seven veils of Nasirism) (Beirut: Dar al-Qadaya, [?1975]).
3. The most complete response by al-Hakim is contained in his *Watha'iq fi Tariq 'Awdat al-Wa'i* (documents on the road to the return of consciousness) (Beirut: Dar al-Shuruq, 1975). This 139-page book is Tawfiq Bey's contribution to the "opening of the file". It contains a number of original documents of which the first is a letter of 26 April 1970, from Tawfiq al-Hakim to President 'Abd al-Nasir calling on him to preserve the independence of *Al-Ahram* and indicating that the Egyptian people do not trust the official media. For more on *Watha'iq*, see Richard Long, *Tawfiq al-Hakim: Playwright of Egypt* (London: Ithaca, 1979) p. 115.
4. Nahman Bar-Nissim, "Tawfiq al-Hakim: The Dramatist" (unpublished Ph.D. dissertation, University of Pennsylvania, 1970) pp. 31–2.
5. (The return of spirit); see below, p. 18, n. 47.
6. (The people of the cave.)
7. 1 May 1964.
8. *Al-Ahram*, 26 May 1967.
9. 5 June 1967.
10. Introduction to his translation of *"Fate of a Cockroach": Four Plays of Freedom* (London: Heinemann, 1973) p. vii.
11. Ibid. Basic biographical information on Tawfiq al-Hakim can be found in his autobiographical works *Zahrat al-'Umr* and *Sijn al-'Umr* (the prison of life; 1964). Excellent summaries, heavily relied on in this work, are: Bar-Nissim, "Tawfiq al-Hakim: The Dramatist", pp. 10–37; 'Awad, *Aqni'at al-Nasiriyah al-Sab'ah*, pp. 1–19. Long, *Tawfiq al-Hakim: Playwright of Egypt*, constitutes an important new source in English; see especially (pp. 112–16) his summary of *'Awdat al-Wa'i* and his views on "whether or not it was a volume to be proud of".
12. John K. Cooley, *Christian Science Monitor*, 22 March 1972, p. 23.
13. *Bird of the East* (Beirut: Khayats, 1966); this introduction was translated with some omissions into Arabic as an introduction to a re-edition of *'Usfur* (Iqra' series, no. 389 [Cairo: Dar al-Ma'arif bi-Misr, 1974]).

14. In this connection see my remarks on the differences between the two Arabic editions of *'Usfur min al-Sharq* and the French version, *L'Oiseau d'Orient* (Paris: Nouvelles Editions Latines, 1960), in the introduction (pp. xi–xiv) to my translation cited above (note 13).

NOTES TO "THE RETURN OF CONSCIOUSNESS"

1. Literally "the abode of books", the title of the Egyptian national library.
2. Now a luxury resort hotel.
3. A station (and surrounding neighbourhood) on the electric tramline from central Alexandria to the affluent eastern section of Alexandria, al-Raml (Ramleh). Bulkeley contained the former British summer residency, was the summer seat of the government when the court moved to the summer palaces of Ra's al-Tin and al-Muntazah. Bulkeley was named after one of the promoters of the tramway.
4. The famous *pâtisserie* on Sulayman Pasha Square.
5. There are two main roads between Cairo and Alexandria, one through the delta which, because it passes through many communities, is considerably slower and the other through the desert west of the delta.
6. On Isma'il Shirin, see P. J. Vatikiotis, *The Modern History of Egypt* (New York: Frederick A. Praeger, 1969) p. 377.
7. Mustafa al-Nahhas (1879–1965). Al-Nahhas, a lawyer by profession, took over the leadership of the Wafd, the main Egyptian nationalist party, in 1927 following the death of its founder, Zaghlul. Elected prime minister on various occasions, al-Nahhas also headed the Egyptian government from 1942 to 1944. On that occasion a British ultimatum backed by tanks and troops imposed al-Nahhas on King Faruq as prime minister. This incident turned a rift between king and prime minister into a chasm. Along with corruption by senior party officials, it also destroyed the moral authority of the Wafd party. The party was banned after the revolution.
8. Hafiz 'Afifi (*b*. 1886) was an early member of the Wafd. In 1938 he published *'Ala Hamish al-Siyasah* (on the margin of politics), in which he criticized politicians for their short-sighted view of Egypt's problems and advocated a programme of positive social action.
9. Published in 1942 and translated into French in 1950, "Pygmalion" is based on the legends of Pygmalion and Narcissus. In the play, Pygmalion carves a beautiful statue which at his request Aphrodite brings to life. Living, Galatea, the statue, is all too human, and again at his request Aphrodite changes Galatea back to stone. In the end Pygmalion destroys the statue. For a detailed outline of the plot see the unpublished Ph.D. dissertation, "Tawfiq al-Hakim: The Dramatist" (University of Pennsylvania, 1970) by Nahman Bar-Nissim, pp. 137–82.
10. (News of the day); Al-Hakim worked at this daily from 1943 to 1951.
11. Born in Alexandria in 1908, Tawfiq Diyab was a prominent capitalist and industrialist.
12. (The struggle); this paper was important during the 1930s.
13. See above p. 2, n.7.

14. Educated at St Johns College, Oxford, 'Abd al-Ghaffar Pasha served as a senator and as minister of agriculture in 1947.
15. Born in 1895, Sulayman Hafiz studied law at Fu'ad I (now Cairo) University. Prior to the revolution he held posts as prosecutor, judge, and counsellor of the court of appeals. He subsequently served as minister of interior (1952–3) under General Najib's government and as vice president of the council of state (1954–8).
16. (The tree of rule); this work first appeared in book form in 1945 but represents, as indicated in the introduction, a collection of shorter pieces published in the press in 1938 and thereafter. In the published form available to me (Cairo: al-Matba'ah al-Namudhajiyah, n.d. [?1968]), it consists of two parts, "Fi al-Akhirah" (in the afterworld) and "Fi al-Dunya" (in this world). The first consists of five wickedly satiric sketches in dialogue form of former imaginary Egyptian men of affairs, each usually with a houri on his arm, who discuss in heaven how they had manipulated people on earth. Part two is a narrative in six brief chapters which tells a similar story emphasizing the foibles and nepotistic practices of a fictional minister newly appointed to the cabinet. The twenty-page introduction outlines al-Hakim's ideas on how the then parliamentary system of Egypt had gone astray and how rule for rule's sake had become the politician's norm.
17. See below, pp. 16 and n. 46, 57 and n. 87.
18. 'Ali Mahir (1883–1960) was a prominent lawyer, landowner, capitalist and politician. He was a member of the Wafd in 1919 but soon after switched to the pro-palace camp. He was a member of parliament from 1924 on, served as chairman of the constitutional committee, and at various times held the portfolios of education, finance, justice, foreign affairs and war. He was also a member of the regency council in 1936 (when King Faruq was a minor) and was prime minister in 1936 and 1939–40. He was forced to resign in 1940 because of pro-Nazi leanings. He also served briefly as prime minister after the 1952 revolution but resigned because of opposition to agrarian reform and to the general direction of the regime.
19. Ahmad Muhammad Hasanayn (1889–1946) emerged on the Egyptian scene after having become known as a desert explorer, diplomat, and in the late 1930s as tutor and close aide of King Faruq. In 1940 he was appointed chief of royal protocol in which post he served until his death in a car accident. As such he was the king's main liaison with political leaders and with British officialdom. Ambitious to protect his sovereign and also to influence the government, Ahmad was a chief *éminence grise* in Egypt during the war years.
20. (Under the sunlight of thought); first published in 1938, *Taht Shams al-Fikr* is a collection of essays.
21. An honorific title of address used for a prime minister.
22. Used for a prime minister.
23. Used for a cabinet minister.
24. Used for a pasha.
25. Used for a bey.

26. A section of Alexandria east of Bulkeley (see above, p. 1, n. 3).
27. ʻAbd al-Razzaq al-Sanhuri (1895–1971). Called by F. J. Ziadeh "the foremost modern Egyptian jurist", al-Sanhuri was the chief architect of the Egyptian, Iraqi, Libyan and Syrian civil codes. He defended democracy, advocated *shariʻah* as the basis for civil law, served in various high posts, and even after the revolution of 1952 headed the council of state. His support for a return to parliamentary life led, at the instigation of army elements, to a mob's attacking him in 1954. For more detail see Farhat J. Ziadeh, *Lawyers, the Rule of Law and Liberalism in Modern Egypt* (Stanford: Hoover Institution, 1968) *passim*. Al-Sanhuri's given name is consistently misspelled throughout the text presumably due to the ignorance of a Beirut compositor.
28. Giza (al-Jizah), an upper-middle-class residential section of greater Cairo on the west bank of the Nile.
29. ʻUmar, one of the greatest Sunni heroes, was the second of the orthodox caliphs (*r*. 632–4). He presided over the early Islamic expansion and the development of nascent Islamic institutions.
30. A Berber freedman, Tariq was the Muslim conqueror (711–12) of much of Iberia. His name is immortalized in the geographical name Gibraltar or Jabal Tariq (the mountain of Tariq).
31. Mahmud Fahmi al-Nuqrashi (1888–1948) was an engineer by profession and originally a Wafdist. He led a militant faction of the Wafd and became a minister as early as 1924 in which year he was also accused of the murder of the British official Sir Lee Stack, but acquitted. Al-Nuqrashi was expelled from the Wafd in 1937, formed the Saʻdist party as a result, and was prime minister twice – in 1945–6 and in 1946–8. He was assassinated while in office by a Muslim fundamentalist.
32. A feddan is slightly more than an acre.
33. Mahmud ʻAzmi (1889–1954), a doctor in law, was a former member of the Democratic Party (of 1918) who joined the Liberal Constitutionalist Party at its inception (1922), edited *Al-Istiqlal*, an inter-war newspaper, and also served as a royal adviser.
34. Saʻd Zaghlul (1857–1927) was the most important Egyptian nationalist leader in the period after the First World War. Born to a peasant family, Saʻd received a provincial religious education and then entered al-Azhar in Cairo in 1871. There he became an intimate of the "modernists", al-Afghani and ʻAbduh. A lawyer, Saʻd was appointed a judge in 1892 and worked assiduously to reform Egyptian institutions, especially legal and educational. He learned French (and later English) and studied at the French law school in Cairo. Through British influence he was appointed minister of education (1906) and minister of interior (1910). In 1913 he resigned and was elected to the new legislative assembly. He now began to emerge as a major opponent of British rule in Egypt. After the war he became the overwhelmingly popular politician, founded and created the Wafd party, and forced Britain to grant independence, somewhat nominal, in 1922. Zaghlul was prime minister from 1923 to 1924 when he resigned rather than submit to the British ultimatum following the murder of Sir Lee Stack. The Egyptian revolution of 1919 resulted from the

British having exiled Zaghlul to Malta. For additional details, see Albert Hourani, *Arabic Thought in a Liberal Age, 1798–1939* (London: Oxford University Press, 1962) pp. 209–21.

35. Named after the prominent hills south-east of Cairo, this newspaper was founded by Faris Nimr and Ya'qub Sarruf, both immigrants to Egypt from Lebanon. Once one of the most important papers in Egypt, *Al-Muqattam* promulgated constitutional reform but was attacked by nationalist activists.
36. The skullcap often worn under the fez.
37. The personalization of a movement such as a revolution is characteristic of Arabic. The usage has been retained in this translation without capitalizing the letter *r*.
38. In 1811 Muhammad 'Ali, the founder of the dynasty of which King Faruq was the last ruler, eliminated the corps of *mamluks*, who had previously ruled Egypt for hundreds of years, by inviting them to a formal dinner at the citadel and there slaughtering them.
39. Best known as the author of *Zaynab* (1913), a novel widely considered (notably by the late H. A. R. Gibb) the first "true novel" in Arabic, Muhammad Husayn Haykal (1888–1956), a lawyer by profession, was also a journalist (editor of *Al-Siyasah*) and an active politician. He served several times as a minister and also (1945–50) as president of the Egyptian senate. He also wrote in the fields of biography and literary criticism. For additional information, consult Ḥamdī Sakkūt, *The Egyptian Novel and its Main Trends from 1913 to 1951* (Cairo: The American University in Cairo Press, 1971) pp. 11–18 and *passim*.
40. *Kalilah wa-Dimnah* is the Arabic version of the fables of Bidpai, a work originally written in Sanskrit, then translated into Pahlavi, thence into Arabic by 'Abd Allah ibn al-Muqaffa' (*ca*. 720–57). The Arabic version, perhaps the earliest bellettristic work in Arabic, was a fabulistic mirror for princes, and is considered a masterpiece of Arabic literature, and forms the basis for further translations into major world languages.
41. Adolf Grohmann (*b*. 1887) was an Austrian Orientalist who made a special contribution to the study of Arabic papyri and Arabic paleography. He worked, *inter alia*, on the South Arabic inscriptions recovered by Philby, Ryckmans and Lippens in 1952 and was a professor at Cairo University and, later, at the Academy of Sciences in Vienna.
42. 'Amr ibn al-'As al-Sahmi (*ca*. 572–663). 'Amr was one of the political and military geniuses of early Islamic history. He played an important role in the Arab–Muslim conquest of Syria and commanded the Muslim armies that conquered Egypt and Libya from the Byzantines. For many years he was the governor of Egypt. For additional detail see A. J. Wensinck, "'Amr b. al-'Āṣ", *The Encyclopaedia of Islam*, New edition, vol. I (Leiden: E. J. Brill, 1960) p. 451.
43. Etienne-Marie-Félix Drioton (1889–1961). Drioton, born in Nancy, took orders and studied theology at the Gregorian University in Rome. He then returned to France and pursued Oriental studies at the Ecole des hautes études and at the Ecole du Louvre. He was named professor at the Institut catholique de Paris in 1920 and was sent to the Institut français d'archéologie du Caire, 1924–6. On his return to Paris he became adjunct

curator in the Egyptian department at the Louvre. In 1936 the Egyptian government appointed him director general of antiquities and of museums. He also became a professor at the Egyptian institute of Fu'ad I University – now Cairo University. The revolutionary regime dismissed him in 1952, and he returned to France, where he held various academic posts culminating (1957) in a professorship at the Collège de France. Drioton was an active archaeologist and a prolific scholar – a major figure in Egyptology. For additional details see D'Amat, Roman and R. Limouzin-Lamothe (eds), *Dictionnarie de biographie française*, vol. 11 (Paris: Librairie Litouzey et Ane, 1967).

44. According to other sources 'Abd al-Malik Sa'd was under-secretary not minister. He served both in 1966 and in 1968.
45. Sidqi received a bachelor's degree in agriculture and was minister of agriculture, 1953–6. As of 1959 he was the regional representative of the UN Food and Agriculture Organization.
46. A reasonably close reading of the version of *Shajarat al-Hukm* available to me (see above, p. 8, n. 16) did not uncover these expressions although on p. 14 the words "*al-'asifah al-mubarakah*" (the blessed storm) occur. Long, *Tawfiq al-Hakim: Playwright of Egypt*, p. 43, indicates "blessed revolution" does occur. Given the shuffling of materials among radio interviews, articles in newspapers and in magazines, and chapters of books characteristic of al-Hakim (and of his period in general), it may be that they appeared in some form or other. On this tendency see Ramsis Awad, "Studies in Contemporary Arabic Literature, I: Tawfik Al Hakim" (unpublished typescript [n.d.] pp. 20–1).
47. *'Awdat al-Ruh* (the return of spirit) was first published in 1933 and probably constitutes al-Hakim's most important and famous novel. Symbolically this story of middle-class Cairo life plays on the Egyptian myth of Isis and Osiris to set al-Hakim's theme that the revolution of 1919 under the inspiration of Zaghlul constituted the return of national spirit to Egypt after centuries of fragmentation. The title, *'Awdat al-Wa'i* (*The Return of Consciousness*), of the book here translated recalls the famous earlier title. For further analysis of *'Awdat al-Ruh*, see Neville Barbour, "'Audatu'r Ruh – an Egyptian Novel", *Islamic Culture*, IX (1935) pp. 487–92, and Sakkūt, *The Egyptian Novel*, pp. 85–9 and *passim*.
48. (The prison of life); this book, published in 1964, constitutes al-Hakim's formal autobiography. It is exceptionally frank in describing his parents. He maintains that everyone is a prisoner of heredity but that in the realm of thought there can be an escape.
49. Al-Hakim here uses two terms, *tahlil* and *takbir*, with heavy overtones; respectively, they also mean saying "*la ilaha illa Allah*" (there is no god but God) and "*Allah akbar*" (God is greater), two of the most emotion-laden Muslim rallying cries.
50. 'Abd al-Nasir's work *Falsafat al-Thawrah* appeared in more than one translated version, including *The Philosophy of the Revolution*, Book I (Cairo: Dar al-Ma'arif, 1954) and *Egypt's Liberation: The Philosophy of the Revolution*, 2nd printing (Washington: Public Affairs Press, 1956).
51. See *Egypt's Liberation: The Philosophy of the Revolution*, pp. 76ff. The

exact language quoted by Tawfiq al-Hakim does not seem to occur in 'Abd al-Nasir's work.

52. Born in 1923 Haykal is, in the West, the most prominent Egyptian journalist. Earning his reputation as a military correspondent in the first Arab–Israeli war (1948), in the Korean war, and elsewhere, Haykal became (1954) editor of *Akhir Sa'ah* and then (1957) editor-in-chief of *Al-Ahram*. During the period of 'Abd al-Nasir, Haykal's weekly column was widely read and considered a reflection of official policy – not least because he was a close confidant of the president, whom he had first met during the 1948 war. He also served as minister of national guidance, 1969–70, and is the author of several important books including, in English, *The Cairo Documents* (New York: Doubleday, 1973), *The Road to Ramadan* (New York: Quadrangle Books, 1975) and *The Sphinx and the Commissar* (New York: Harper & Row, 1978). Since the death of 'Abd al-Nasir, Haykal has found no official favour. For a well-informed sketch, see Edward R. F. Sheehan, "Introduction: The Most Powerful Journalist in the World, His Newspaper, His Book", in Haykal, *The Cairo Documents*, pp. xi–xxxv.
53. These two sentences occur respectively on pp. 15 and 18 of the introduction to *Shajarat al-Hukm*.
54. A conservative Egyptian politician of Turkish background, 'Adli Pasha (1864–1933) was a co-founder of the Liberal Constitutionalist Party which represented aristocratic and intellectual circles but had little popular support. A minister in the government at the time of the formation (1918) of the Wafd, 'Adli was only nominally opposed to Zaghlul. He formed a government briefly in 1921, again in 1926–7, and lastly as an independent in 1929.
55. (The pyramids); a Cairo daily. Founded in Alexandria in 1875 by Salim and Bisharah Taqla, youthful immigrants from Lebanon, *Al-Ahram* moved to Cairo in 1900 and became Egypt's leading paper. It was nationalized after the revolution of 1952 but has continued to play a major role.
56. I have deliberately changed the text here in two places. Al-Hakim erroneously wrote *L'Observateur* instead of *L'Exprès* and Schreiber for Servan-Schreiber (*b*. 1924). The latter, whom he doubtless intended, is the well-known journalist and man of affairs who has served his country as minister and deputy and who has written a number of important books, perhaps most notably *Le Défi américain* (1967).
57. The Arab Socialist Union, of which President 'Abd al-Nasir was the leader, was founded under the terms of the draft national charter of 1962 as the single legal political party in Egypt. It succeeded two earlier such parties, the Liberation Rally and the National Union. It was hierarchical in nature starting at the village level and ending with a supreme executive council. Its representatives were powerful at all levels and its mission was, *inter alia*, to establish broad national policies.
58. The word for "victor" is *nasir*.
59. A prominent engineer with a Ph.D. from Birmingham University, Dr 'Abd al-'Aziz Ahmad was in 1947 the director of the department of electrification of the Aswan reservoir. In the mid-1950s he spoke out

against the construction of the High Dam. Prior to the 1952 revolution he had served as a senator.

60. On the White Nile, 29 miles above Khartoum where a dam creating a large annual storage reservoir was built. Construction was completed in 1937.
61. Sir William Willcocks (1852–1932) was an outstanding water engineer, with prior experience in India, who joined the British administration of Egypt in 1884, in which year he successfully repaired the Nile barrage below Cairo. In 1894 after four years of field work in Upper Egypt Willcocks proposed that a dam be built across the First or Great Cataract of the Nile. This, the first dam at Aswan, was designed by Willcocks and completed in 1902. He also worked on irrigation projects in Iraq. In his time Willcocks was blessed in local mosques for his benign works, and a street is named after him in the al-Zamalik section of Cairo. Willcocks was also a prolific author.
62. ‘Abd al-Nasir and the world (Beirut: Dar al-Nahar, 1972).
63. Hilmi Bahjat al-Badawi (*b.* 1904) was a prominent Egyptian lawyer and also a professor of law. He received the doctor of law degree from the University of Paris, joined the revolutionary regime in 1952, served as minister of state for foreign affairs and as minister of commerce and industry. As of 1954 he became the chief Egyptian delegate to the board of the Suez Canal Co. and was instrumental in the preparation of the legal case for nationalization of the canal in 1956. He was appointed (26 July 1956) first chairman of the newly created Suez Canal authority.
64. An independent conservative politician, Sirri (*b*. 1892) served as prime minister on three occasions, 1940–2, 1949–50, and 1952. His third government lasted only 18 days and led directly to the revolution of 23 July 1952.
65. For a summary account of Egypt's involvement in Yemen see Tom Little, *Modern Egypt* (New York: Frederick A. Praeger, 1967) pp. 198–216.
66. A member of the dynasty of Muhammad ‘Ali that ended with King Faruq's abdication in 1952, Isma‘il (1830–95) ruled Egypt from 1863 to 1875. He was an extensive and effective modernizer who, however, was extravagant and was deposed at least in part because of serious financial difficulties.
67. (The perplexed sultan); this play, first published in 1960, tells the story of a just sultan who upholds principle and law in the face of personal humiliation. It has been translated into English as "The Sultan's Dilemma", and can be found in Tawfik Al Hakim, *"Fate of a Cockroach": Four Plays of Freedom*, trans. Denys Johnson-Davies (London: Heinemann, 1973).
68. (Bank of fear); this play written in 1967 implied that the regime of ‘Abd al-Nasir was socialist in name only and that fear was widespread in Egypt. The word *qalaq*, here translated as *fear*, implies *upset*, *terror*, *Angst*.
69. Conqueror.
70. Victor.
71. Thunderbolt.
72. Al-Badawi (*b.* 1887) received law degrees from Toulouse and Grenoble

and became professor of international law at Cairo University and also a member of the university council. He was, as stated, a judge in The Hague.

73. The Institut was created by Napoleon in 1798. Its mission was to make a comprehensive study of Egypt and to make policy recommendations to the French regime. The Institut survived the French withdrawal from Egypt. For a sympathetic summary, see Vatikiotis, *The Modern History of Egypt*, pp. 39–41; for a harsh view, see Edward W. Said, *Orientalism* (New York: Pantheon Books, 1978) pp. 83–7.
74. Gaspard Monge (1746–1818) was a prominent mathematician considered to be the inventor of descriptive geometry. Among other applications this new approach had a special value in the siting of forts. He accompanied Napoleon to Egypt and was involved in matériel and strategic decisions. Monge served as minister of marine, 1792–3, and was a builder and democratizer of the prestigious Ecole Normale Supérieure and Ecole Polytechnique.
75. Mu'awiyah ibn abi Sufyan (*d.* 680) was the founder of the Umayyad dynasty which ruled the caliphate from 661 until 750. He was an astute military and political leader who initiated dynastic rule in the Islamic state.
76. Ahmad 'Urabi Pasha (*ca.* 1840–1911) was a military officer of peasant origin who became the leader of the nationalist forces in 1879. By 1882 Colonel 'Urabi had become the *de facto* leader of Egypt. His brief moment was ended by the British occupation of Egypt in that same year, and he was exiled.
77. Son of Khedive Isma'il (see above, p. 37, n. 66), Tawfiq (1852–92) became khedive in 1875. He was a weak ruler torn between the rising forces of Egyptian nationalism and European imperialism. During the British invasion of 1882 he sought the protection of British guns and was thereafter paid scant attention by the real rulers of Egypt.
78. The period before Islam and hence, for Muslims, a time of ignorance.
79. Al-Sharqawi, an attorney, was educated at Cairo University and received the doctor of laws degree from the University of Paris. He was professor of law at Cairo University and also practised law for a while in Kuwait. It is widely accepted that al-Sharqawi was brutally tortured following his arrest in 1966 (he was imprisoned for 15 months) on a charge of having established illegal contacts with the Muslim Brethren while abroad. The case was publicized in 1968, and it was alleged that al-Sharqawi's confession was forced.
80. Originally from Manufiyah province, 'Abd al-Rahman al-Sharqawi (*b.* 1920) is best known as a novelist. His works emphasize rural life and peasant customs. Of these his novel *Al-Ard* (the earth) is considered the best. In the 1960s he interested himself in Islamic socialism and wrote the well-known *Muhammad Rasul al-Hurriyah* (Muhammad the messenger of freedom).
81. Al-Qalali was a professor of criminal law at Cairo University. During the defence of al-Sharqawi, al-Qalali charged that heads of the general intelligence service were responsible for the torture. It was ruled that the confession had been secured in a lawful manner; however, Salah Nasr, chief of the intelligence, resigned in 1967.

82. See above, p. 9, n. 27.
83. Taha Husayn (1889–1975) is along with Tawfiq al-Hakim one of the best-known modern writers in Arabic. Blind from the age of three, he studied at al-Azhar, at Cairo University, and in Paris, where he received his doctorate in classics. Prominent as a critic, novelist, translator, essayist, historian, travel writer and autobiographer, Taha Husayn was also a professor, rector (of Alexandria University) and minister of education. His works have been translated into many languages, and his honours were numerous. André Gide wrote, concerning Taha, of the "patiente victoire de la lumière spirituelle sur les ténèbres" (quoted in Vincent Monteil, *Anthologie bilingue de la littérature arabe contemporain* [Beirut: Imprimerie Catholique, 1961] p. 129).
84. 'Abbas Mahmud al-'Aqqad (1889–1964) was another of the important Egyptian writers of the generation of Taha Husayn and Tawfiq al-Hakim. Not formally educated beyond primary school, al-'Aqqad moved from his birthplace, Aswan, to Cairo at fourteen. He learned English well and turned to journalism. Literary criticism and biography were perhaps his fortes although among his 70-odd works nearly every form of written expression including the novel and verse were essayed.
85. See above, p. 18, n. 47.
86. See above, pp. 55 and 18, n. 47.

———— # ————

87. In *'Awdat al-Wa'i* the word is *jā'i'ah* (hungry), but in the original, in *Shajarat al-Hukm*, p. 14, it is *jā'ihah* (devastating). Presumably, the original was mistranscribed in *'Awdat al-Wa'i*.
88. This passage appears on pp. 14–15 of the introduction to *Shajarat al-Hukm*.
89. An informal title of respect. The reference here is to Muhammad Hasanayn Haykal.
90. The author refers to the Suez war of 1956 in which Great Britain, France and Israel invaded Egypt. The trigger for it was 'Abd al-Nasir's nationalization of the Suez Canal company.
91. *Sultan al-Zalam* (the power of darkness) is a collection of essays which first appeared in 1941. The contents include pieces reflecting on the destiny of humanity and defending spiritual and intellectual forces. The subject of another, hence the title, is the road to liberation from the power of darkness.
92. Abu Za'bal is a large prison predating the 1952 revolution and named after the district in which it is located on the outskirts of Cairo.

Index

A few proper names or events are not indexed because they occur on almost every page. These include *'Abd al-Nasir, Egypt, Egyptian,* and the *1952 revolution*.